GASLIGHTING

A Recovery book to recover from emotional abuse

Myra Nelson

This page is intentionally left blank

This page is intentionally left blank

Table of Contents

INTRODUCTION

Gaslighting which is a detailed and insidious technique of deception and psychological manipulation, generally practiced by a traitor or "gaslighter" for a victim for a long time. Its purpose is to gradually undermine the victim's confidence in his own ability to distinguish the truth from the lie, directly from the lie or from the reality of appearance, which makes him pathologically dependent on a gas lighter in his thinking or his feelings.

As part of this process, the victim's self-esteem is severely compromised, and he or she also becomes dependent on the gaslighter for emotional support and validation. In some cases, the expected (and achieved) result is to deprive the victim of his health.

The phenomenon is highlighted in the clinical literature as a form of narcissistic abuse in which an extreme narcissist tries to satisfy his pathological need for assurance and constant appreciation ("narcissistic supply") by transforming vulnerable people into intellectual and emotional slaves which he paradoxically despises—their victims. Because the gaslighter itself is usually psychologically disturbed, it is often not fully aware of what it's doing or why it is doing it.

The term is derived from the British scene of 1938 under the title gas light, which was later produced in the form of a film, gaslight, in the united kingdom (1940) and the united states (1944). These dramas vividly, if somewhat simplistic, describe some of the basic elements of the technique. These may include: trying to convince the victim of the truth about something intuitively strange or outrageous by demanding it strongly or by organizing superficial evidence; categorically deny that someone said or did something that is clearly said or done; reject the victim's opposite perceptions or feelings as unworthy or pathological; questions the information and motivations of those who contradict the views of the gaslighter; gradually isolate the victim from independent sources of information and validation, including others; and manipulate the physical environment to which encourage the victim to doubt the veracity of their memories or observations. For example, in plays and films, a deceptive husband leads his wife almost to madness by assuring her that she is a kleptomaniac and that she has imagined only the sounds of the attic and the low dimming of the lamps gas from the house which were, in fact, the result of missing precious stones from his aunt.

This exercise manual, separated into three sections, was made to bring the psychological mistreatment strategy known as gaslighting out beyond all detectable inhibitions. Part I investigates how to perceive indications of gaslighting, comprehend the objectives of the individuals who utilize this strategy seeing someone, and recognize ways gaslighting may appear in changed connections and situations.

A few activities are intended for helping you recognize your own

encounters with gaslighting and create self-compassion to start your I am recuperating venture.

Parts II and III will walk you through activities and prompts intended to assemble confidence, increment self-assuredness, build up limits, and assemble more advantageous connections. Through and through, this exercise manual will assist you in setting up a strong comprehension of how gaslighting actually works, how to spot it, and how to recoup.

While jumping directly to the activities might be enticing, I unequivocally urge you to begin toward the start and also work your way through each area altogether, as every section expands on the past. You may discover a few activities upsetting, while others you might need to return to a few times.

Kindly don't surrender. Once in a while the main way out is through and recuperating is a work-through-it sort of try. Be patient and kind to yourself.

On any off chance that you end up feeling completely overpowered, damaged, or pitifully stuck in your mending procedure, think about looking for extra help. Recuperating from psychological mistreatment is difficult to work. A gifted and merciful specialist can offer magnificent help.

An amazing asset for controlling others, gaslighting can be utilized to stifle or kindle entire networks inside a bigger society. Numerous pioneers and legislators depend vigorously on gaslighting to substitute certain gatherings or actuate their own supporters with the slanted manner of speaking. Since these characters can be enchanting and charming, they can use a noteworthy impact. With a sufficient after, a horde like an attitude can create—one that can successfully quietness any individual who ventures outside the imperceptible lines.

While people with certain personality disorders, for example, a narcissistic personality disorder, marginal personality disorder, and solitary personality disorder (otherwise called sociopathy), are more liable to participate in gaslighting to control others, this strategy isn't exclusively in the area of narcissists and sociopaths. People without personality disorders may likewise participate in gaslighting, despite the fact that not continuously for similar reasons. Perceiving this as misuse can be hard at first, and getting out troublesome practices you find in a cozy relationship significantly harder. We expect those nearest to us to think about our prosperity, and a specialist gaslighter can cause you to accept the victim is harming you for your own great.

As you become increasingly mindful of gaslighting over various settings what's more, connections, you may feel overpowered—possibly sad. Overcomers of psychological mistreatment frequently battle with sentiments of self-question, loss of certainty, nervousness, and discouragement, just to give some examples. Luckily, there is trust. You can figure out how to perceive the indications of gaslighting, and you can recoup from the harm.

On any off chance that you perceive yourself in the accompanying pages, it would be ideal if you realize that recuperation is workable for you, as well. In perusing, you will extend your comprehension of this tricky type of psychological mistreatment, learn concrete abilities to shield yourself from falling casualty once more, and start to recuperate the injuries of the past. The mental fortitude and steadiness of my customers have roused me to concentrate on supporting overcomers of gaslighting, narcissistic maltreatment, also, enthusiastic control. I am everlastingly thankful to them for making a difference me find my energy for this work. Presently it's your chance to proceed the inheritance of mending.

Things being what they are, you've chosen to look for a specialist to enable you to mend? Congrats! Be that as it may, also where do you start? While looking for the correct specialist, think about such. Factors as permit, instruction, helpful modalities, claim to fame and cost. I suggest scanning for an authorized psychotherapist, proficient guide, therapist, or clinical social laborer who spends significant time in recuperation from Psychological mistreatment as well as harmful connections.

The Internet can be a helpful apparatus to locate the opportune individual to help. Various online vaults list clinicians by area and territories of claim to fame. The Resources which segment at the end of this book likewise has a rundown of national libraries. In the event that you'd like to have an individual suggestion, ask friends or relatives or your essential consideration specialist.

Finding a specialist who feels like a solid match for you by and by is vital. Numerous clinicians offer a short, free phone counsel before booking an underlying meeting.

Try not to be very hesitant to get some information about their experience helping customers recuperate from gaslighting and harmful connections. What's more, recall: It's alright to be particular. You have the right to locate the opportune individual to help you in your venture.

CHAPTER ONE

Gaslighting

Gaslighting includes an individual, or a group of people, the offender, and a subsequent individual, the victim. It very well may be either cognizant or oblivious and is completed secretively with the end goal that the subsequent psychological mistreatment isn't plainly harsh.

Gaslighting relies upon "first persuading the casualty that his reasoning is twisted and furthermore convincing him that the lowlife's thoughts are the right and genuine ones." Gaslighting incites intellectual disharmony in the victim, "frequently sincerely charged psychological discord," and makes the victim question their own reasoning, discernment and perception. In this manner they, in general, drive in them low confidence, distressing thoughts and influences. They may also incite the development of disarray, nervousness, melancholy and at times even psychosis. After the victim loses trust in their intellectual abilities and builds up a feeling of learned defenselessness, they become increasingly powerless to the offender's control. Victims will, in general, be individuals with less force and authority.

The role of either offender or victim can sway inside a given relationship, and oftentimes each of them is convinced that they are the target victim. At the point when a group is the victimizer, gaslighting does its harm through the group "Little, frequently imperceptible activities that have power through their aggregation and reinforcement." Gaslighting has been utilized by people and groups for "achieving relational and social command over the spiritual working of others and groups."

The deceptive truth impact is a wonder wherein an audience comes to think something principally on the grounds that it has been rehashed so regularly, which may happen to a casualty during gaslighting.

Psychoanalytic clarification

In a 1981 article, psychoanalysts Victor Calef and Edward Weinshel contended that gaslighting includes the projection and introjection (the "move") of a psychological medium from the gaslighter to the gaslighted victim. The psychological medium includes affects, recognitions, driving forces, protections, dreams, hallucinations, and clashes. The creators investigated an assortment of reasons why the victims may tend "To consolidate and absorb what others externalize and project onto them." They inferred that gaslighting might be "A complex exceptionally organized design which includes commitments from numerous components of the mystic contraption."

Afterwards, specialist Theodore Dorpat depicted this "move" of the offender's unconscious psychological abuse, for instance of projective personal proof. For recognizable projective proof to be best, the casualty would be ignorant of being gaslighted. It becomes ruinous when the casualty relates to the substance of the "move" (what has been anticipated). These impacts are dropped when the casualty is fit for doubting and misidentifying with the negative introjects that outcome from recognizable projective proof.

In personality disorders

Sociopaths and narcissists as often as possible use gaslighting strategies to mishandle and undermine their casualties. Sociopaths consistently violate social mores, overstep laws and exploit others. Moreover, they are usually persuasive liars, and at times, very enchanting ones, who constantly deny bad behavior. Subsequently, persons who have been exploited by sociopaths may question their own thinking. Some truly harmful partners may gaslight their own partners by blatantly denying that they have been violent.

Gaslighting may happen in parent-child relationships, with either parent, child, or both misleading the other and attempting to undermine thoughts.

In psychiatry

Gaslighting has been seen among patients and staff in inpatient mental offices.

In a 1996 book, Dorpat asserted that "gaslighting and different techniques for relational control are generally utilized by emotional well-being experts just as others" since they are compelling strategies for molding the conduct of others. He noticed that disguised techniques for relationship control, for example, gaslighting are utilized by clinicians with dictator attitudes, xiii–xxi and he suggested rather more non-order and democratic mentalities and strategies with respect to clinicians, "regarding patients as dynamic teammates and equivalent accomplices".

In romantic connections

In romantic relationships, the offender "should be right" so as to "save [their] own feeling of self," and "[their] feeling of having power on the planet"; and the victim allows the gaslighter to "characterize [their] feeling of the real world" because of the fact that the victim "romanticizes [them]" and "looks for [their] affirmation".

The mental control may include the formation of the victim questioning their own memory, perception, and rational soundness. The victimizer may invalidate the victim's experiences by using cavalier language: "you're insane. Try not to be so delicate. Try not to be jumpy. I was simply kidding! ... I'm stressed; I believe no doubt about it."

Analysts Jill Rogers, and Diane Hollingshead said that such excuses could be unfavorable to psychological well-being effects. They portrayed mental abuse as "scope of aversive practices that are expected to hurt a person through pressure, control, insufferable attack, checking, seclusion, undermining, desire, mortification, control, regarding one as a substandard, making an unfriendly domain, injuring an individual in regards to their sexuality and additionally constant, dismissal of a partner sincerely as well as truly."

Gaslighting has been seen now and again of conjugal unfaithfulness: "advisors may add to the casualty's misery through mislabeling the [victim's] responses. [...] The gaslighting practices of the life partner give a formula to the supposed 'mental meltdown' for some [victims] [and] self-destruction in a portion of the most noticeably awful circumstances."

In their 1988 article "gaslighting: a marital syndrome," analysts Gertrude Zemon Gass and William Nichols examined men's extramarital undertakings and their results on their spouses. They depicted how a man may attempt to persuade his better half that she is imagining things instead of admitting to an issue: "a spouse gets a phone augmentation in her own home and coincidentally catches her significant other and his sweetheart arranging a tryst while he is on a work excursion." His disavowal challenges the proof of her detects: "I wasn't on the phone with any sweetheart. You were more than likely dreaming."

Rogers and folding stand inspected women's encounters with mental abuse as an indicator of side effects and clinical degrees of despair, anxiety, and distress, just as self-destructive ideation and life functioning. They inferred that mental abuse influences women's emotional wellness effects, however, the apparent negative changes in one's qualities, risky relationship constructions, and reaction styles were more grounded markers of psychological well-being effects than the real abuse.

Psychotherapist Stephanie Moulton Sarkis clarified that it takes "A specific measure of psychological discord to stay associated with a gaslighter" and that "The most beneficial approach to determine cognitive dissonance" in such circumstances includes "Leaving or separating yourself from the gaslighter."

Signs and techniques

As depicted by Patricia Evans, seven "cautioning signs" of gaslighting are the watched abuser's:

1. Denying information of the victim;
1. Countering information to fit the victimizer's point of view;
2. Limiting information;
3. Utilizing insufferable attack, as a rule as jokes;
4. Blocking and occupying the casualty's consideration from outside sources;
5. Trivializing ("limiting") the victim's worth; and
6. Sabotaging the victim bit by bit by debilitating them and their manners of thinking.

Evans thinks of it as essential to understand the warning signs so as to find a way to recover from it. The analyst Elinor Greenberg has portrayed three common techniques of gaslighting:

1. **Hiding**. The victimizer may hide things from the victim and hide what they have done. Rather than feeling taking responsibility, the victimizer may persuade the victim to question their own convictions about the circumstance and turn the fault on themselves;

2. **Evolving.** The victimizer wants to change something about the victim. This may be the manner in which the victim dresses or acts, they need the victim to fit into their dream. If the victim doesn't agree, the victimizer may persuade the victim that he or she is incompetent;

3. **Control.** The victimizer may need to completely control and have control over the victim. In doing so, the victimizer will attempt to separate them from other loved ones so no one but they can control the victim's thoughts and actions.

The victimizer gets joy from realizing the victim is to a great extent, completely controlled by them.

A victimizer's definitive objective, as portrayed by the separation procedure mentor Lindsey Ellison, is to have their victim re-consider their decisions and to scrutinize their logical thinking, making them progressively reliant on the victimizer. One strategy used to debase a victim's confidence is the victimizer switching back and forth between dominating and taking care of the victim, so the victim brings down their desire for what comprises friendship and sees themselves as less deserving of warmth.

Role of gender

Humanist Paige Sweet, with regards to social disparities and power, close relationships filled with aggressive behavior at home, has expected gaslighting strategies that "Are gendered, in that they depend on the relationship of gentility with unreasonableness."

As indicated by Philosophy Professor theorist Kate Abramson, the demonstration of gaslighting isn't explicitly attached to being misogynist, despite the fact that ladies will, in general, endure powers of gaslighting in contrast with men who all the more frequently take part in gaslighting. Abramson clarified this because of social construct and said, "It's a piece of the structure of sexism that ladies should be less certain, to question our perspectives, convictions, responses, and observations, more than men. What's more, gaslighting is planned for subverting somebody's perspectives, convictions, responses, and recognitions. The misogynist standard of self-question, in the entirety of its structures, sets us up for simply that." Abramson said that the last "stage" of gaslighting is extreme, major, clinical sadness. With regards to women specifically, Philosophy Professor Hilde Lindemann said that in such cases, the victim's capacity to oppose the control relies upon "Her capacity to confide in her own decisions." Foundation of "counterstories" may help the victim reacquire "common degrees of a free organization."

Psychotherapist Stephanie Moulton Sarkis, who observed gaslighting to be existing in around 30–40% of the couples she treats, says that "Gaslighting is as liable to be finished by men as ladies" and that "Supposedly, the sexes are spoken to similarly." She clarifies further that we will, in general, believe gaslighters to be for the most part men since "Men are frequently increasingly hesitant (maybe humiliated) to converse with somebody about a female partner who is by and large truly damaging."

In parent-kid connections

Youngsters on account of cruel parents may become victims of gaslighting. Maternal gaslighting of little girls has received particular attention. In a segment named "lying, gaslighting, and denial" in her blockbuster Mothers Who Can't Love: a healing guide for daughters, specialist and writer Susan forward states: "A seriously narcissistic mother's outrage, analysis, and neglectful excusal of her girl's emotions are difficult and damaging. What's more, every girl sticks to the conviction that if her mom could just see that behavior and its effects, she'd stop. Girls attempt over and over to hold up a mirror, trusting that this time, things will be unique. However, serious narcissists remain exactly as expected, reacting to any showdown with dramatization followed by redirection and attention on your inadequacies. At the point when that doesn't deliver the ideal outcomes, they go to what exactly might be their generally baffling and enraging device: forswearing. The encounter causes them to feel cornered, and when that occurs, they can't and won't approve your experience or recognize their part in it. Or maybe, they revamp reality and disclose to you that what you saw, you didn't see, what you encountered didn't occur, and what you call genuine is really an invention of your creative mind."

Be that as it may, both moms and fathers may gaslight kids. Mentally abusive parents often openly put on a "great parent" face, yet hold back love and care in private. This drives youngsters to scrutinize their own view of the real world and to ponder whether their parent is the acceptable individual everyone else sees, or a lot darker individual that comes out when child and parent are separated from everyone else. Manipulative guardians may likewise "set youngsters in opposition of one another; ... Play favorites, and, convince the disliked child that everything is their fault for not being progressively talented, prettier, and in any case increasingly adorable."

In politics issues

Editorialist Maureen Dowd was one of the first to utilize the term in a political setting. She portrayed the Bill Clinton organization's utilization of the method in oppressing Newt Gingrich to slight insults proposed to incite him to submit open questions that "seemed to be crazy."

In his 2008 book State of Confusion: Political Manipulation and the Assault on the American Mind, analyst Bryant Welch depicted the predominance of the strategy in American governmental issues starting in the period of present-day exchanges, expressing: To state that gaslighting was initiated by the Bushes, Lee Atwater, Karl Rove, Fox News, or some other surviving group isn't just off-base, it also misses a significant point. Gaslighting comes legitimately from mixing present-day agreements, promoting, and publicizing procedures with long-standing strategies for proclamation. They were essentially holding on to be found by those with adequate aspiration and mental cosmetics to utilize them.

Writer Frida Ghitis utilized the expression "gaslighting" to portray Russia's worldwide relations. While Russian agents were dynamic in Crimea, Russian authorities consistently denied their quality and controlled the doubt of political groups in support of themselves.

Columnists at The New York Times magazine, BBC and Teen Vogue, just as therapists Bryant Welch, Robert Feldman and Leah McIlrath, have depicted a portion of the activities of Donald Trump during 2016 US presidential political race and his term as president as instances of gaslighting. Journalism professor Ben Yagoda wrote in the chronicle of higher education in January 2017 that the term gaslighting had become effective again as the consequence of trump's conduct, saying that trump's "constant propensity to state 'x,' and afterwards, at some later date, angrily proclaim, 'I didn't state "x." Actually, I could never fantasize about saying "x" had carried new remarkableness to the term.

Gaslighting is used by leaders and supporters of political groups to guarantee similarity of any possibly going amiss individuals.

In the working environment

Gaslighting in the working environment is when individuals do things that cause partners to address themselves and their activities in a manner that is hindering to their professions. The casualty might be barred, made the subject of gossip, vigorously ridiculed or addressed to obliterate their confidence. The victimizer may redirect discussions to saw blames or wrongs. Gaslighting can be experienced by anybody and can be particularly inconvenient when the offender has a place of intensity.

In mainstream society

The 2016 mystery and suspenseful thrill ride movie The Girl on the Train investigated the immediate impacts gaslighting had on the hero (Rachel). During her marriage, Rachel's ex Tom was a vicious victimizer and offender. Rachel experienced intense unhappiness and alcohol abuse. Whenever Rachel would pass out intoxicated, he constantly revealed to her the awful things she had done that she was unable to recollect.

Gaslighting was the principal topic of a 2016 plotline in BBC's radio drama, The Archers. The story focused on the psychological abuse of Helen Archer by her partner and later spouse, Rob Titchener, throughout the span of two years, and caused a lot of open conversation about the topic.

For a while during 2018, gaslighting was a principle plotline in NBC's drama Days of Our Lives, as character Gabi Hernandez was found gaslighting her closest friend Abigail Deveraux after Gabi was arrested for a homicide Abigail had submitted in the arrangement.

In March 2020 the Dixie Chicks discharged a tune named "gaslighter," the title track from their future collection gaslighter, a reference to gaslighting propelled by lead artist Natalie Maines' separation from on-screen character Adrian Pasdar.

CHAPTER TWO

The Gaslighter

In this section, we will profile people generally known for gaslighting. This type of psychological abuse is usually connected with mental illness, for example, a narcissistic personality disorder, borderline personality disorder, and avoidant personality disorder. The Diagnostic and, Statistical Manual of Mental Disorders, fifth edition (DSM-5, 2013), characterizes a personality disorder personality disorder as "an enduring pattern of internal experience and behavior that goes astray extraordinarily from the desires of the person's way of life." Problematic characteristics and practices are enduring and broken. Accordingly, these people both endure also, cause agony to other people, disturbing their lives and connections. A few people may exhibit characteristics that don't meet measures for an emotional wellness analysis. A valuable term for not-exactly diagnosable people is nearly insane people. Nearly insane people can engage, control, and menace with the best, yet avoid a genuine mental sickness. Anybody can be harsh, yet not every person who misuses has a personality disorder.

An abuser profile

Gaslighting can be an indication of a some personality disorder.

As indicated by the National Institute of Mental Health, about nine percent of adults meet the requirements for a personality disorder finding. Despite the fact that gaslighting is not an away from of a personality disorder—and a lot of gaslighters try not to have an emotional well-being analysis—people with (analyzed or not) personality disorders are probably going to work on gaslighting in numerous connections.

Here, we will concentrate on gaslighting as an expansion of certain, all the more regularly analyzed personality disorders.

What is a narcissistic personality disorder

A personality disorder is a variety of enduring personality traits across relationships and situations, causing suffering and distress in those relationships. People with narcissistic personality disorder often express qualities like a disposition of self-importance, excessive need for appreciation, absence of sympathy and understanding, a constant need for approval, and a conviction that they are special and deserving of special treatment. Furthermore, they are coercive, engage in manipulative practices, and have a propensity to intimidate others to get their own way.

Those with this personality disorder exploit others, controlling and using the individuals around them for their own advantage. Narcissists may use gaslighting to keep up their own feeling of predominance by keeping others in an weakened position. Numerous, political figures and CEOs are high in narcissistic traits. These power figures may utilize gaslighting to either arouse their admirers or stifle their control, seeking after their own plans to the detriment of others. Borderline personality disorder is portrayed by elevated mood instability, exceptional fear of dismissal, precariousness in relationships, and a feeling of emptiness at their core. This disorder also includes a propensity to cycle among romanticizing and depreciating friends and family, pulling them closer and driving them away. People with borderline personality disorder go to extraordinary lengths to maintain a strategic distance from genuine or saw deserting, including undermining to hurt themselves if their accomplice attempts to leave. They may use gaslighting to cause others to feel answerable for the gaslighter's government assistance.

For this situation, gaslighting is less about attempting to deliberately control someone else and more about attempting to meet the borderline individual's own need to have a sense of safety.

Some other sociopathic disorders

Those with antisocial personality disorder and psychopathy are also likely offenders of gaslighting. Antisocial personality disorder, sometimes referred to as sociopathy is described by disregard for or abusing, the rights of others. Sociopathic people don't adjust to accepted practices. Most often, their method of gaslighting includes either lying or deceitfulness, and they may direct destructive behavior toward outsiders as opposed to friends and family.

In spite of the fact that the terms are used conversely, sociopathic what's more, psychopathic attributes vary in force and focusing on. Persons with sociopathic tendencies are more averse to intentionally focus on those nearest to them, while those with psychopathic traits are prone to display hazardous behaviors to family, friends, or outsiders. Psychopaths are also indifferent to the effects of their actions; they are incapable of compassion or regret. They may actually enjoy harming others.

Objectives of gaslighting

Victimizers use gaslighting to control their victims, overall surroundings and types of relationships. Five obsessive objectives of gaslighters are:

- Hindering discernment in the victim: Gaslighting creates uncertainty and disarray for the victim. Since the victim addresses their own judgment and perceptions, they may find it difficult to separate right from wrong, solid from undesirable, their viewpoint from their victimizer's point of view. Gaslighting makes victims have a feeling that they can't confide in themselves to observe the reality of a circumstance. They become increasingly more subject to the gaslighter for a "reality check," which just serves to propagate their disarray;

- Silencing the victim: Gaslighting can be a successful instrument to silence someone by making them question their own credibility. Victimizers will lessen the influence and reach of their victim's voice through lying and defaming. They may persuade the casualty that nobody will trust them since they (the victim) are such a problematic observer;

- Building up a sense of entitlement over the victim: Victimizers control victims into surrendering their own existence, compelling them to accept the victimizer's version of events. Gaslighters displace their victim's perceptions with their own by utilizing "selective realisms." Gaslighters do not value their victim's perspective. Rather, they value feeling like the leader, being appreciated, and in charge. Victimizers bulldoze their victims since they feel qualified to transform another person's world as opposed to questioning their own.

Manipulating and chastising the victim

Gaslighters may manipulate and degrade victims by portraying their victim responses to abuse as childish or juvenile.

Chastising a victim for responding to agitation suggests that the shortcoming lies with the victim, not the victimizer. Victimizers may likewise manipulate their victims by brushing off the victim's achievements or accomplishments. The gaslighter may reprimand the victim for being proud, proposing that if the victim worked sufficiently hard, they would really have something to show that is truly worth being proud of: Legitimizing their treatment of the victim. Gaslighting can be utilized to persuade the victim that the victimizer's cruel behavior is justified. As confidence in their own resources diminishes, they become progressively dependent on and tolerating of the gaslighter's presence. What's more, when a victim accepts that they deserve the treatment they receive, they become more averse to opposing or challenging harmful actions. Furthermore, the gaslighter may persuade themselves that they are being cruel for the victim's benefit and that this treatment is supported.

- Composing exercise: Psychological abuse through gaslighting is successful in light of the fact that it deliberately obstructs the victim's thinking, self-sufficiency, and self-efficacy.

The five objectives recognized put the gaslighter in more control of their victim.

How have the gaslighter (s) in your life sought after these objectives in your relationship? Expound on your encounters with every one of their five objectives.

- Normal phrases used by a gaslighter: The following are a few basic gaslighting phrases in the event that any solid recognizable, place a check in the contiguous box;

- "I wouldn't have said that if you hadn't provoked me." Here, the gaslighter diverts fault onto the victim. The objective is to make the victim accept that they brought the abuse upon themselves;

- "You intentionally confused what I said." This state throws fault on the victim for not reading the gaslighter's mind and infers that the victim distorted the gaslighter's "true" aim;

- "You know how I feel about that, and you did it, anyways, so the manner in which I've responded is your own shortcoming." This expression suggests the victim alienated the gaslighter, supporting their harmful behavior accordingly;

- "That never occurred." Denying a victim's recollections furthermore, experiences confounds and confuses them. Gaslighters likewise ruin victims to others by denying occasions or professing to have no memory of them;

- "You sound insane." Dismissing somebody's opinions or beliefs as sounding impractical, triggers self-question and anxiety in victims;
- You're trying to confuse me." This allegation switches the situation of the victimizer and victim, making the true victim apprehensive;

- "I have no clue about what no doubt about it." Claiming not to comprehend a victim's anxiety proposes that their experience is so out of the ordinary, it's ambiguous. The victim at that point addresses whether they are imagining things or if their memory is distorted;

- "You're not remembering right." This expression infers that the victim's recollections and observations are faulty, raising doubt about their judgment;

- "I am just hard on you because I love you." This expression is utilized to induce gratitude and forgiveness in victims. Victimizers guarantee to put stock in "strong but fair affection," or "Coming out with the plain truth," paying little mind to the effect on the other individual;

- "You are too delicate. You have to grow a thicker skin." Perhaps one of the most treacherous expressions in the gaslighting list, the intention behind these words it to raise doubt about the victim's right to their own emotions. If the victim is "excessively touchy," the responsibility is on the victim to figure out how to endure the abuse, rather than on the gaslighter to stop what they're doing.

Understanding what is gaslighting behavior

Now that you're acquainted with the signs and objectives of gaslighting, you'll be better prepared to abstain from falling victim to it later on. Looking back at your past and seeing the control in a relationship you once thought was love can be hard. You may ask why you were unable to see through the control at that point, and why you needed to endure such a great amount of torment previously, you understood what was truly occurring. You may feel harmed, broken, or on the other hand, moronic for having been deceived. Be sympathetic to yourself. Being targeted by a damaging character isn't a character imperfection.

Victimizers target victims dependent on one of two things: weakness and attractive quality. Some gaslighters search for victims who are willing to disregard dependent treatment and injurious behavior. They target individuals who need to be seen as agreeable and easy to be with; these people are less inclined to incite the gaslighter and are all the more effectively controlled.

There is such a mind-boggling concept as being too pleasant, and gaslighters will take the opportunity to control such victims.

Victimizers may likewise target people who seem unquestionable, prolific, rich, or alluring. They are attracted to strong, confident individuals. Controllers attract individuals through a procedure called "love bombing"— giving potential victims friendship, approval, and fake intimacy. When victims are entrapped, the gaslighting starts and victimizers start to break the confidence that previously attracted them to their target.

A gaslighter profile

Are some personality types progressively helpless to being gaslit than others? While victimizers target victims for various reasons, numerous victims share a few qualities practically speaking.

Numerous gaslightees are accommodating people, excessively concerned with being cooperative, pleasant, or popular. They are reliable, worried about others' emotions, and may feel guilty saying "no." Finally, gaslightees are probably going to pardon or neglect inconsiderate and pernicious behavior exorbitantly.

Do you fit the gaslightee profile? Complete the self-examination underneath:

Self-test for gaslightee. Rate how evident each statement is for you by circling t "often ," "sometimes," or "rarely. "

> **1.** Contradicting, somebody feels like I am "beginning dramatization." I will attempt to

maintain a strategic distance from these sorts
of circumstances.

Often

Sometimes

Rarely

1. I feel pressured that I will offend someone on if
   I say "no" to them.

   Often

   Sometimes

   Rarely

2. I regard others' decisions more than my own.

   Often

   Sometimes evident

   Rarely

3. If I am progressing nicely and my partner isn't, I
   feel like my achievement is hurting them.

   Often

   Sometimes

   Rarely

4. I have an inclination that I ought to be more in
   charge of my feelings.

   Often

Sometimes

Rarely

If you selected "often" to more than three questions, you might be in more danger of being gaslight.

Keep in mind that your voice and judgements matter, and it's alright to state "no." You reserve the right to be treated with respected.

Phases of recovery

Recovery from psychological mistreatment is a procedure. Much like building a house begins with laying a strong foundation, recuperation from gaslighting starts with coping with the painful reality that you have experienced abuse in a relationship. In stage one of your recovery, there's affirmation and self-compassion, one must distinguish, examine, and deal with the ways gaslighting has presented itself in your life. The road to recovery starts with identifying the presence of an injury, followed by building up an attitude of generosity toward yourself.

CHAPTER THREE

Stage One (Acknowledgement, What's More, Self-Compassion)

Since we have laid the foundation, you are prepared to start your journey to gaslighting recuperation. We've discussed what gaslighting is, the means by which this behavior may show up in different settings, what's more, what makes gaslighting harmful to someone. We have also identified the signs and symptoms of gaslighting, and what prompts individuals to utilize this damaging strategy. Now it's your turn. You will begin to examine and identify the ways gaslighting has affected you.

This section contains various activities and programs to assist you with understanding control in disastrous relationships. The first step in your recovery is observing, and allowing yourself to acknowledge that you've been a survivor of gaslighting. Accepting reality by identifying what's happened can help clarify a difficult experience. The first few parts of this chapter will focus on helping you through this process as you assess past and current relationships.

Accepting you have experienced psychological abuse may introduce feelings of shame. Gaslighting affects your confidence and damages your self-awareness. Hence, figuring out how to practice self-love is crucial to your recovery. Self-empathy is an outlook.

With self-compassion, you offer yourself thoughtfulness, understanding, and acknowledgement of the torment you have endured, without scrutiny or self-blame.

Beating yourself up for being controlled won't help you with fixing the damages of an harmful relationship. Bringing thoughtfulness and sympathy to the parts of you that have been harmed will.

Perceiving manipulation

Do you know gaslighting when you see it? In the following scenarios, you will be given have three attempts to identify elements of gaslighting in real-life settings. Examine each story carefully, and try to identify the signs,, and responses of gaslighting in each situation—review the "signs of gaslighting" and "symptoms of gaslighting" covered in part 1, if required.

Squashed hopes

Julia is eager to move into her first school dorm and start an independent, adult life. She enthusiastically reveals to her mother, her arrangements to play intramural sports. "I feel truly prepared to begin something new!" she spouts. When her mom giggles so anyone might hear, Julia is squashed.

"Goodness, nectar," she says condescendingly. "You realize you aren't athletic enough for sports."

Julia feels her energy and confidence drift away. She had thought intramurals would be a great method to build up another ability, however, now she isn't so sure.

"Apologies, mom. I guess you're right. I was most likely being ridiculous. I guess a thanks is in order for the rude awakening."

Distinguish the signs and side effects

1. Indicate some signs of gaslighting in this relationship.

____

____

____

____

____

2. Identify   the symptoms of gaslighting Julia is experiencing.

____

____

____

____

3. Have you at any point encountered a friend or relative gaslighting your feelings, abilities, or decisions? Expound on this experience here.

____

____

____

____

____

Allegation boomerang

Andre has found a flirtatious and explicit texts between his partner, Ben, and another man. Andre and Ben have had this battle numerous times before. Andre is hurt and enraged. He confronts Ben. He tells Ben that the relationship is over, and he is moving out.

"I can't believe you are so emotional over two or three text messages," Ben whines, sounding appalled. "I am not undermining you. You're simply seeing what you want to see. Why are you so untrustworthy?

You love to be the victim, and I'm not going to tolerate it. You don't get to control me." Ben puts some distance between him and Andre, the image of injured pride. Andre is crushed.

"Ben, I didn't mean to blame you for cheating. I just got so annoyed when I saw the texts. I'm sorry I accused you. I simply need us to be straightforward with one another." Andre puts his arms around Ben and murmurs a humble, "I'm sorry. I love you." Ben goes to Andre and hugs him back. "I forgive you."

Identify the signs and side effects

1. Identify some of the signs of gaslighting in this relationship.

____

____

____

____

____

____

____

2. Identify some symptoms of gaslighting that Andre is experiencing.

____

____

____

____

____

____

____

3. Have you at any point in life experienced gaslighting by a romantic partner? Expound on this experience here.

____

____

____

____

____

____

____

Vulnerable population gaslighting

In spite of the main fact that anyone can be affected by psychological abuse, some people are more likely to suffer from such abuse. People who identify as asexual, genderqueer, eccentric, or transgender have more risk factors, as their abuse can be intensified by existing cultural beliefs and power structures. LGBTQ people might be gaslighters by others scrutinizing their "weirdness," precluding use from claiming the right pronoun or persuading them they deserve abuse due to their sexuality and sex personality.

Gossiping office

Sasha is anticipating her up and coming final assessment. She has settled down in her new position and it has been worthwhile. She has a decent relationship with her director, Felicia, and left their pre-evaluation meeting with a positive feeling. Felicia even indicated the plausibility of a performance based raise.

When Felicia calls Sasha into her office to go over the assessment, Sasha is stunned and disheartened by Felicia's notes: "Sasha's overall performance is disappointing. She doesn't put in invest much effort yet feels qualified for a raise. Sasha needs to rethink her goals and improve her hard-working attitude if she wants to advance in this organization." As she examines the remarks, Sasha feels confused and embarrassed.

She thinks about whether she was adding something more to Felicia's prior remarks about a conceivable raise, and if she made herself look eager by appearing too excited at the possibility. Afterwards, she catches two directors from different divisions examining her. Felicia has disclosed to them that Sasha requested a raise and complained about her associates. The gossip is fanning out quickly, and Sasha ends up completely disregarded by associates.

Recognize the signs and side effects

1. Identify some indications of gaslighting in this passage.

____

____

____

____

____

____

2. Identify some symptoms of gaslighting that Sasha is experiencing.

____

____

____

____

____

3. Have you at any point experienced gaslighting in the working environment? Write about this experience here.

____

____

____

____

____

Identifying the signs in real life

Review the "signs of gaslighting" section in part 1. Compose a model of how each sign has appeared in your life. It's alright if your experiences don't actually correspond with the settings in the list (e.g., you may have been harassed by a friend or scapegoated by families).

I have been the subject of ridiculous gossip.

I have been constantly undermined.

I have been relied upon to speculate what someone might be thinking.

I have been dealt with deceptively.

I have experienced deception.

I have been blatantly deceived.

I have been undermined.

I have been forced to isolate myself from loved ones.

I have been tormented or threatened.

I have been blamed for a malignant plan where there was none.

I have been caused to feel blameworthy.

I have been treated like I was blowing things out of proportion.

____

____

____

I have been caused to feel like my sensible solicitation to another was difficult or uncalled for.

____

____

____

____

____

I have been accused and humiliated.

____

____

____

____

Identifying your side effects

Review the "symptoms of gaslighting" found in chapter 1.

Compose a case of how every one of these reactions has appeared in your life.

I have needed assurance or had low confidence.

____

____

I have experienced unhappiness or lost enjoyment.

____

____

____

____

I have wound up saying "sorry" for things outside my own control or for circumstances in which I reserved an option to say "no."

____

____

____

____

I have felt indecisive.

I have felt confused.

I have been burdened with self-question.

I have been unwaveringly anxious.

____

____

I have been consciously ignorant of another's gaslighting behavior.

____

____

____

____

I have felt discouraged.

____

____

I have felt amazingly driven.

____

____

____

Reward: If any of the listed symptoms used to be applicable but aren't anymore, what has changed? Expound on how you were able to improve.

____

____

____

____

Well hindsight is 20/20: reviewing past incidents
Examining past occurrences of gaslighting can assist you with remembering them later on. Illustrate a period in which you experienced gaslighting. Identify the thoughts and emotions you experienced at that point, as well as any lingering thoughts and emotions you occasionally have.

Choose an instance of gaslighting in your life. Expound on this involvement with as much detail as possible.

How did you feel when the gaslighting circumstance occurred?

____

____

____

____

____

What is your opinion about this occurrence now?

____

____

____

____

What type of thoughts did you have at that point?

____

____

____

____

What type of recollections do you have about this occurrence now?

____

____

____

____

If you experienced this situation today, what might you need to do in an unforeseen way? Compose how you might want to react having found out about gaslighting.

____

____

Duplicate the former two pages and rehash this activity as frequently as you'd like. What's more, don't spare a moment to return to an occasion more than once. You may learn new things about the corresponding or comparative conditions by rehashing the activity.

Where have I actually seen this behavior before? Make a list of movies, tv shows, plays, or books where you can identify gaslighting. Are there any you wouldn't have seen before reading this book?

____

____

____

____

____

____

Your body in space

Pause for a minute to examine your body. How do you stand? Do you stand tall, or on the other hand, are your shoulders drooped? Do you make yourself as little as possible around others, or would you say you are happy with your body?

Men, ladies, and genderqueer people have experienced gaslighting identified with their physical bodies through social media, advertising, and maybe different types of settings. Maybe you were content with your body until your social media feeds out of nowhere are laden with shapewear promotions. Or maybe, you were content being thin until you got assaulted with advertisements for protein powder and working out programs. Absence of mainstream society and media portrayal (or distortion) of people with physical difficulties, of color, or with a sexual personality that changes from the standard can communicate something specific about types of individual personality and self-expression that are socially acceptable, and those that are depicted as a freaks, non-conforming, or cartoons.

Think back about what you have been told about your body and physical looks Answer the questions below to explore ways you may have experienced gaslighting with regards to your body.

When I think about my body and my appearance, I feel.

____

____

____

____

____

Where did I learn how to think about my body?

____

____

____

____

____

Something I acknowledge and love about my body (regardless of whether somebody suggests I shouldn't) is:

____

____

____

____

____

At the point when your body speaks, listen

Did you realize that horrible experiences can influence our bodies, not simply our brains? In his original work, The Body Keeps the Score (2014), Dr Bessel Van Der Kolk investigates ways an injury can make changes to how the cerebrum works, change sensory system excitement, and cause long term torment also, incessant illness. Your body doesn't separate between an injury that originates from military battle or psychological abuse, for example, gaslighting. Injury is injury, and our bodies can recount to the story of our intense suffering. As we go through this section and start to concentrate on self-consolation, remember your body. Focus on physical feelings that may emerge as you go through this book. Strong migraines, illness, exhaustion, a fast-beating heart, and tightly held hands are all markers of injury being communicated through your body. Although awkward, these physical sensations are giving you more information about how and where the injury is in your body.

Suppressed feelings introspection

Find a place that feels calm, serene, and safe. Sit in an comfortable position. You may close your eyes if you wish, or keep them open. Allow your mind to relax into the center . Focus your attention on your breath and your physical nearness. At the point when your thoughts drift, identify them and come back to your inner core focus. Now think about a memory encompassing gaslighting or another intense abuse. Try not to go directly to your most distressing memory; pick one that feels modestly unbearable. Allow the memory to surface, and grasp as many details as you can. Don't take too much time exploring this memory. Start to observe the feelings that emerge. Pick one that feels strong and allow your inner self to carefully concentrate on that feeling. Name the feeling, saying something like "This is an outrage," or "This is melancholy." Try not to pass judgment on your emotions.

Next, allow your concentration to move to your physical self. Push out your body from the top of your head to the bottom of your feet. Keep focusing on the feeling you distinguished already. Ask your body to take you to where the feeling is held.

At the point when you discover the feeling, place a hand delicately on the area where you notice the sensation. Envision sending a rush of love to that place as you state, "I offer myself compassion for my indignation," or, "I offer myself compassion for my anguish." Notice how your physical and inner selves respond to your compassion. Do they relax? Stand up to? Keep on sending compassion until you feel conditioning. Thank your body for showing you how it holds this feeling. If you'd like, interact with your body in a soothing course by giving yourself an embrace, extending your arms to the roof, or rubbing your neck.

Exercise self-talk

Have you at any point observed the manner in which you talk with yourself about yourself? The way we think and talk with ourselves is called self-talk. Self-talk can be thoughtful, empathetic, and positive, or cruel, critical, and negative.

What does your self-talk sound like?

____

____

____

____

____

Gaslighting can negatively affect self-talk and self-perception.

In this area, we will examine how your self-talk reflects your convictions about yourself. The following situations are intended to assist you with changing negative, critical self-talk to generosity and self-compassion

Exercise self-description

You can acquire the ability to competent in your self-talk by giving close thought to the types of words you use to portray yourself to yourself. Here, check it out.

Portray yourself in five words or expressions.

____

____

____

____

____

____

What type of words did you choose? Did you portray yourself in positive, negative, or impartial terms? In the event that you focused on what you consider to be negative traits, at that point, your self-talk is likely negative.

Attempt the activity once more, this time underlining self-compassion language. For instance, rather than portraying yourself as "excessively passionate," try "receptive to my emotions," or "suitably sensitive."

Let's adopt it to your best friend

Imagine you are listening to your closest friend talk about a time when they were gaslit. Imagine that they disclose to you that they feel inept for letting themselves be controlled, and they dread never being able to recover from the abuse. What is your response to them? Presently envision giving yourself the equivalent thoughtfulness. Compose your reaction here.

Psychological abuse is not gendered

As per the national domestic violence hotline, almost half all things considered and men (48.4% and 48.8%, separately) experience mental abuse by a partner during their lifetime. While a great majority of the investigation and overview of psychological abuse in the media is introduced as men taking advantage of women, men can likewise be gaslit by female partners, friends, family members, and associates. There is likewise an added social humiliation for men who have been abused, as being betrayed might be viewed as a shortcoming. As recently noted, genderqueer people can likewise be the both victims and victimizers of psychological abuse. Nobody is invulnerable.

Self-compassion journal

Keep a diary of everyday occasions that offer chances to practice self-compassion.

For every occurrence, note the following three approaches:

1. Thoroughly consider. What occurred, and how did you feel about it? Try to be non-critical and non-condemnatory as you note your feelings.

2. Standardize your response. Compose a line or two about how your response is similar other people's response. For instance, numerous individuals become baffled when another driver cuts them off in rush hour gridlock. Being puzzled is an ordinary reaction.

3. Offer self-benevolence. Compose a couple of lines offering yourself empathy, consolation, and solace. Attempt to be thoughtful and sensitive.

What occurred, and what was my opinion about it?

____

____

____

____

How is my response consistent with that of other people?

____

____

____

____

I can give myself grace by:

____

____

____

____

Complete this activity day by day for in any multi-event week and observe how you feel toward the end of the week.

A good letter of self-forgiveness

Numerous survivors of abuse battle with self-blame. They believe they could have averted the abuse by behaving differently, ending the relationship sooner or leaving and not going back. Do you blame yourself for anything identified with your abuse? Assuming this is the case, write yourself a sort of letter offering yourself forgiveness. Be explicit about what you forgive yourself for and refrain from setting conditions on your forgiveness.

____

____

____

____

____

____

Disguised gaslighting

If you are experiencing problems with giving yourself mercifulness and compassion, examine the purposes for your uncertainty.

Observe if your self-talk incorporates messages like "You

have the right to be gaslit in light of the fact that you were too dumb to even think about seeing what was occurring," or, "Well, he was correct, you are a lethargic lazy pig. In the event that you just tidied up on occasion, he wouldn't have any motivation to state that."

These messages are a sign of disguised gaslighting, which can happen when you have become so accustomed to psychological abuse that you turn cruel words and distortions on yourself, once in a while as a type of self-defense.

Gaslighting yourself may make it you more odd for you to show the sort of confidence and decisiveness that prevents further abuse from the other individual in your relationship. Disguised gaslighting is likewise a way that abuse can proceed even when a victimizer isn't truly present. If you see yourself along these lines of reasoning, the next exercise will be particularly important.

Attestations

Work on checking negative self-thoughts with attestations. Observe if this task is difficult and ask yourself what feels unpleasant or wrong. I urge you to bear it, regardless of whether you find this activity hard. Accepting that you are deserving of rewarding yourself with affection and sympathy is an outlook that must be learned and refined.

Here are a few examples of confirmations that advance self-compassion:

"I have the right to be treated with respect."

"I don't have the right to be controlled and abused."

"I have sympathy for the parts of me that have been harmed by oppressive relationships."

"I acknowledge the part of myself that needs to accept the best in individuals and may forgive fearsome behavior."

"I am deserving of affection and empathy."

In this activity, you will make a dream board which speaks to your journey toward self-compassion.

On one side, the montage will have pictures, words, fascinating covers, and different materials that speak to a relationship represented by gaslighting. The relationship can happen in any situation (familial, individual, work, romantic, and so forth). The words and pictures you pick ought to outline the disarray, absence of self-assurance, anxiety, and, other responses you experienced in that relationship.

On the opposite side, you can speak to your post-gaslighting self. This board ought to outline your mindfulness and self-compassion. Create a picture that addresses your responsibility to recover from abuse. If you are still battling to let go of the gaslighter's effect, think about your second side as a positive. How would you like to see yourself?

Put your vision board in an noticeable spot so you can get everyday reminders of how far you've come!

Part with it

On a piece of paper, write down a word, expression, memory, or picture related to your gaslighting experiences. Examine your note, and then, cover the paper up as little as possible under the circumstances. Discard the paper by discharging it to one of the components—cover it in the earth, shred it and toss it to the wind, glide it out to the ocean, or consume it (securely!). As you discharge the words, state to yourself "I don't have to convey this gaslighting with me any longer."

____

____

____

____

____

Show self-compassion

You may wind up still battling with letting go of your gaslighter's behaviors and personal attacks. If you find self-compassion hard to deal with, that is alright. Start by discussing your hope of being kinder to yourself. When you put your goals out into the universe, you are empowering your goals to become active inside you.

Compose a statement showing adoring compassion for yourself. Expression your statement as a current activity—regardless of whether you're attempting to associate with the cherishing generosity.

Model: "I make space in my heart for self-compassion. I welcome

thoughts from myself and to myself."

Audit and wrap-up

Review the activities in this section. What impacted you the most?

____

____

____

____

____

What didn't resound?

____

____

____

____

How would you feel at this moment? How have your emotions changed since you have you begun this section?

____

____

____

____

What will you take away from these activities?

____

____

____

____

____

____

CHAPTER FOUR

Building Self-Esteem

Welcome to stage two in your recovery—where you will begin to repair the damage done to your confidence. In the first two sections, we looked at some examples of gaslighting and the impacts of this type of abuse on victims. In section three, we examined the signs and side effects of gaslighting for you, ultimately, and started forming self-compassion.

Now we will proceed with your recovery journey by rebuilding your confidence and creating self-assurance.

Section four has activities and journal tasks aimed at helping you identify the damage to your confidence from toxic relationships and learn ways to be your brave and stand up for yourself in relationships. Some sections of your recovery include understanding and practicing various styles of correspondence, ways to appreciate yourself more and reinforcing an attitude of development and appreciation.

Some of these activities will feel hard. It very well may be hard to think decidedly about yourself in the wake of having been gaslit into believing you were close to your imperfections. Show restraint toward yourself. Gaslighting would not be as compelling at controlling individuals without the waiting impacts. Take your time and be thoughtful to the pieces of yourself that battle with these Works out.

Self-assured bill of rights

Numerous survivors of psychological abuse battle with standing up for themselves seeing someone. They have been adapted to see supporting themselves as an indication of self-centeredness. That is an untruth.

Coming up next is an assertive bill of rights, adapted from Manuel J.

Smith's "A bill of assertive rights" (1975). Examine each of the following items, and note how you feel:

I reserve the option to pass judgment on my own thoughts, emotions, and practices, regardless of any other individual's evaluation of them.

I reserve the right to my thoughts and sentiments without expecting to legitimize or apologize for them.

I reserve the right to adjust my perspective.

I reserve the right to say "no" without feeling apologetic.

I reserve the right to make mistakes, and the responsibility to address them when they happen.

I reserve the right to say, "I don't have the foggiest idea."

I reserve the right to say, "I couldn't care less."

I reserve the right to take up physical, mental, and emotional space.

I reserve the right to feel empathy for somebody without being responsible for fixing them.

I reserve the right to settle on the best decision for me, regardless of whether this decision. Isn't favorable to someone else.

I reserve the right to frame my own grouping of qualities, moral code, and morals, free of others.

I reserve the option to separate or decide not to connect with people who are unpleasant to me.

I reserve the option to leave a toxic relationship, regardless what kind.

I reserve the option to be my own individual, with all the one of a kind and extraordinary individualities that make different from others the individual on this planet.

Composing exercise

How do you feel as you read each line of the assertive bill of rights?
What resonated and what didn't? Did any of the rights feel especially difficult to acknowledge or concur

with? Compose your response(s) to the assertive bill of rights here.

____

____

____

____

Provide particular concerns to the rights that were hardest to acknowledge. Those will address puts most needing improving.

What is self-esteem, and why is it very significant?

Self-esteem alludes to your own feeling of worth and esteem. Your degree of self-esteem has a noteworthy and direct influence on how you conduct yourself around someone and how you hope to be deal with. In the event that your self-esteem is excessively low, you believe you don't have the right to be treated with affection and respect. You naturally accept others are above you.

You are bound to accept abuse since you don't believe you're deserving of anything better. If your confidence is excessively high, you might be pretentious, egotistical, and have ridiculous desires to be viewed as extraordinary. You may believe yourself to be above others.

Irrational self-esteem can be a part of a narcissistic personality. The tragic absurdity is that a few narcissists really feel deeply unworthy, and their pretentiousness, gaslighting, and social climbing are generally some kind of an attempt to feel more significant.

With proclaimed confidence, you can value your qualities, identify your imperfections and assume responsibility for your mistakes without believing that they adversely influence your motivation as an individual. You can expect satisfactory treatment in relationships and feel free to leave destructive or on the other hand, oppressive behavior. You can show individuals how to treat you, and that starts with how you treat yourself.

Fixing the damage

Obsessive victimizers create victims by working on their confidence after some time. Luckily, what was chipped away can be rebuilt. The following activity looks at how to identify the ways in which your self-esteem was harmed and teach you methods to start repairing.

- Stage one: write down or draw an image indicating a word, expression, or behavior that was used to gaslight you;
- Stage two: write down or draw an image demonstrating how this word, expression, or on the other hand, behavior from stage one triggered you to think about yourself;
- Stage three: write or draw an image of a possible belief about yourself to assess the gaslighter's implication. Now say this belief out loud. Observe how you feel about yourself as you say your new message.

Closest friend bio

Imagine that your closest friend has been approached to add to your account. The victim will be asked details about who you are as an individual and what makes you unique. The description will concentrate on your unique personality traits, individual achievements, abilities, and qualities. Compile one section about yourself through the eyes of your closest friend. The following questions are proposed cues, but are original!

The main prerequisite is that you center around the positive characteristics.

Your closest friend celebrates.

Recommended talk with cues:

What might your closest friend say makes you unique?

What qualities and skills do you have?

Shouldn't something be said about you is your closest companion generally pleased with?

What does your closest companion accept most about you

____

____

____

____

Reward option

Sit down with your closest friend and use these questions to direct a honest meeting. Compose your friend's responses here.

____

____

____

____

Qualities survey

We as a whole have unique qualities, skills, and personality traits that make us special. If for a while, you haven't considered the characteristics that make you different from everyone else, now is your opportunity: in this activity, lay out everything that is phenomenal about you.
Consider the things you like most about yourself, regardless of whether it's personality traits or skills you've developed over your lifetime.

Well, this isn't an ideal opportunity to be modest. This is an ideal opportunity to name and invest passionately in everything that makes you unique!

As you expound on your qualities, skills, and unique characteristics, think about how you've established them over your lifetime. In what way can you develop them further all through?

One thing I like about myself is:

____

____

____

____

One thing I am pleased with is:

____

____

____

____

One thing that is unique about me is:

____

____

____

____

The quality, skill, or characteristic I am generally pleased with myself for is:

____

____

____

____

I discovered this quality/skill/characteristic by:

____

____

____

A superpower that is dependent on my real qualities,
skills, and attributes would be:

____

____

____

I would utilize this superpower along these lines:

____

____

____

The "I love you" exercise

During the last exercise, you may have realized your
inner critic having a few comments about your
qualities, skills, and character traits. If you find it hard

to say anything nice about yourself, this next exercise is particularly for you. You may dislike it—complete it Nonetheless.

Inner critics are the parts of us that have concealed the insensitive and critical expressions we endured in daunting relationships. What we may refer to as "a fussbudget" is basically an inner critic doing everything to keep you from making mistakes. The inner critic is challenging you, not out of dislike, but in an effort to actually assist you, preventing you from turning into the object of further abuse. Your inner critic is trying to safeguard you by making you mindful of your imperfections so you can hyper-redress for them. As it were, behind the unforgiving methodology is a sincere goal.

This activity is tied in with loving yourself, imperfections and all. Self-esteem begins with a single word: self. To like yourself, you must be appreciative toward yourself. Furthermore, that love stretches out even to the parts of you that can be critical of you. This activity will assist you in finding your love for yourself.

"I love you" meditation

Close your eyes and imagine sitting across the table from your inner critic a. Imagine yourself sitting or standing close enough to your inner critic to see its eyes and hear its voice—observe if you feel on edge, sad, angry, or apprehensive. Inhale deeply and slowly, using your abdomen, feeling your midsection extend with every inward breath and pour out with each exhalation. Breathe in harmony, silence, and confidence; let   out any dread, outrage, and uneasiness. Take a look at your inner critic and let it know you are here to have a talk.

Start by advising the critic that you'll listen to what it needs to say now, and that you are prepared to hear what it doesn't like about you. Ask the critic to identify each complaint so that you can be aware of each and alter them as needed. Make a point to check on with your breathing all through the reflection. Keep on breathing slowly and deeply, feeling your breath filling and clearing your lungs as you listen to your inner critic, attempt to stay keen and receptive. Do you feel the voice? How do you feel when you hear something negative about you? Where do you feel the reaction, in or around your body? In the event that you feel stressed, upset, or preoccupied, come back to your deep breathing until you can continue your discussion with the inner critic.

This is important. Each time your inner critic identifies a complaint, stop. Study how you feel and where you feel that reaction. Place a hand on the section where you feel your intense reaction, and state, "I love you." Repeat this cycle after each analysis.

How do you feel as you say "I love you" after each analysis? Does your heart feel still, constricted, or hurt? Place a hand over your heart and state, "I love you."

Keep repeating "I love you" until you feel your heart calm,
warm, and open up laden with affection. When you feel your heart is open and full of adoration, take a look at your inner critic—that part of you that helps you to remember each slip-up and imperfection—and state, "I love you, as well." How does the critic react?

Keep sending adoration to the parts hurt by the scrutiny you have hidden. Send love to your inner critic—the part of you that has remembered these implications—with the goal that you'll never be harmed again. Feel the love in your heart. It's sufficient to cover each wound you've gotten.
Breathe in affection, breathe out torment. Place a hand over your heart and state, "I love you."

I love you meditation can bring up numerous emotions. What did you notice as you finished the reflection? Write your reaction to the practice here:

____

____

____

____

____

Experience positive traits

For the traits recorded below, expound on a time you expressed each of them. How have your positive qualities been useful for you and others?

Mental strength:

____

____

____

____

Compassion:

____

____

____

____

Open-mindedness:

Love:

Kindness:

Intelligence:

Confidence:

Happiness:

Assurance:

Tolerance:

Loyalty:

____

____

____

____

Instinct: ______________________________________

____

____

What's going on with you versus what happened to you

The manner in which you speak with yourself can be a ground-breaking power for self-compassion or on the other hand self-gaslighting, extremely affecting your feeling of self-worth what's more, self-esteem. When you feel bad about yourself, you'll likely think that it's much harder to participate in emphatic thinking.

This activity expands on the compassionate "self-talk exercises" you practiced in part 3. Start by constructing a statement you may as of now use to describe yourself in relation to your experiences. At that point, revise that statement to represent an instance or situation that influenced you, but, doesn't characterize you.

History of growth timeline

Sometimes when we become extremely focused on our imperfections and mistakes, we dismiss the progress we've made. This activity helps track your development in at least one aspect of your life. You may map your progression as mental, passionate, otherworldly, or from your physical ability, or in a specific part of abuse recovery, for example, recovering confidence or increasing willingness to change.

Below, outline a series of events indicating your development and progress in one or more areas.

Keep tabs on your development in the course of the most recent week, month, year, five years, ten years, or more. How has this quality changed as you have developed? How far have you come?

You may likewise note the times you stumbled, got lost, delayed, or backtracked in your progression. Each distinctive part of the development! Be pleased with yourself for overcoming the difficulties.

Making the next stride

After finishing your sequence of events, you may consider making another group of objectives to pursue . Is there a specific skill, interest, or quality you would like to develop? A part of repairing and recovering that supports a more centered methodology?

Think of today as the first step of your next plan for growth.

Where would you like to go from here? Distinguish three to five objectives that you can develop as you push forward in your life. Where do you need to be in a year? Five years? Ten? Think deeply! Anything is possible.

Day by day appreciation

When you wake up, record, in any case, one thing you appreciate about yourself. Take your note, sit or stand in front of a mirror and read the message loudly to yourself, multiple times. Take a look at yourself in the mirror as you talk and don't stress over sounding ridiculous. Place the note in a place where you can see it, and review the message again toward the day's end.

Repeat this activity consistently for 100 days, acknowledging something different about yourself each time. Put an update in your schedule or set an alert on your phone to assist you with ensuring that you put in time each day to appreciate yourself. Keep your notes and put them into a scrapbook or organize a plan with them toward the end of this period

Day by day gratitude

In a similar manner to the "day by day appreciation" activity, end your day by recording, one thing that you are appreciative for.
What you choose can be big or small, noteworthy or insignificant. Set yourself up for rest by taking five minutes to focus on something you feel grateful for.

 Abundance: manifesting self-esteem
Put together five statements or mantras to welcome in and make room for sound confidence and dignity. Below, compose certification ever as though you've

just gotten these blessings of self. Offer appreciation to the universe, or on the other hand, whatever resounds for you deeply, for your wellbeing and recovering.

Models:

"I adore and value myself just as I am."

"I invite a sense of pride and firm self-assurance."

"I express gratefulness for the insight and resilience of my heart."

Your turn:

____

____

____

____

Guarantee your space

Non-verbal communication can uncover a great deal about us. How we sit, stand, and move can mirror our degree of solace with living on earth. This practice allows you to examine what your non-verbal communication says about your self-esteem. You will require sufficient room to loosen up, so find an open area where you can stand. If you can be before a mirror, that would be incredible, but it's okay if you can't. In case you are unable to stand, sit up as straight and tall as possible.

Think about when you felt small, embarrassed, dishonorable, or unhappy with yourself. What does your body look like when you don't hold yourself to high esteem? Do you sit or stand tall? Droop? Are you looking down? Take a moment to focus on your non-verbal communication when you don't like yourself.

Now imagine yourself as confident, decisive, and aware of your esteem. You love yourself and have the right to live on earth.

We should work on guaranteeing your life as a sure, decisive, and worthy individual.

Remain with your feet hip-width apart, arms hanging freely by your sides. On the off potential for success that you can't have, sit up tall with your back as straight as conceivable. Feel your feet immovably in contact with the floor. Your weight ought to be spread equitably between your large toes, pinkie toes, and heels (or solidly on both sit bones in the event that you are situated). Press your feet into the floor and imagine lifting up through your middle simultaneously. Sit or stand serenely straight. Feel tall, solid through your center, and adjusted.

Slightly contract the muscles of your legs, posterior, and upper back.

Try not to grip; your objective is to be aware of the quality of your body. Feel the energy in your muscles. Gently force your shoulder bones back and down. Feel the open space in your chest and over your collarbones. Raise your arms sideways, either at a low corner to corner, shoulder stature or high askew, whichever feels best to you. Raise your chin and look upward on a high corner to corner. Feel energy destroying your arms and out of your fingertips. Feel the space around your heart extend. Guarantee your space.

Raise your arms straight overhead and press your palms together.

Lift your face and look at the sky. Feel your feet grounded on the floor as you move upward and straighten yourself. Guarantee your space.

Bring your arms to chest level, keeping your palms together and bringing down your gaze to look straight ahead. Pull your elbows back and place your hands on your hips, feeling your shoulder bones pulling down and, back once more. Lift your chest slightly, feeling the energy through your shoulders, upper arms, and hands or clench hands as they lay on your hips. Feel your strong physical nearness. Guarantee your space.

Showing assertiveness

Decisive agreement and a self-assured mentality are often the norm. However, finding a fair compromise between being a mat and being a steamroller can be shockingly hard. For recouping passives, a significant number of the limitations to decisiveness lie in their own beliefs about pushing for self-confidence. In this activity, we will examine your thoughts as well as your beliefs about your own self-confidence.

What does assertiveness mean to you?

____

____

____

____

Identify somebody in your life you consider as self-confident. How would they act?

How would you look at them?

____

____

____

____

What advantages do you see to turning out to be progressively emphatic yourself? What may the disadvantages there be?

____

____

____

____

At the point when you imagine yourself talking decisively, what are the "buts" in your self-talk? What feels amazing, harmful, or alarming about attesting yourself?

____

____

____

____

In what capacity may your life change if you turned out to be more confident? Do you think things would improve, or become worse? What are the risks also, rewards of changing?

____

____

____

____

____

____

The benefits of assertiveness

While being assertive can be hard for gaslighting victims, the possible effect is critical. Confident interaction has numerous benefits, including:

• increased assurance and confidence

• decreased pressure

• greater capacity to observe and understand your feelings

• more respect from others

- better interpersonal skills

- more fair relationships

- positive change

- increased feeling of self-growth

At the point when you get drained and begin to focus on why you're buckling down To turn out to be progressively emphatic, record the manners in which these advantages could Improve your life.

____

____

____

____

____

____

Interactive styles

Most interactions can be categorized as one of four general divisions or styles: passive, aggressive, passive aggressive, and assertive. How we interact can have a critical effect on how we are seen by others, and how we act in front of others.

Passive interaction is shy, self-destroying, withdrawn, avoidant, and requires assurance. Passiveness may likewise appear similar to an obliging person or feeling like a mat in relationships. Numerous psychological abuse victims are withdrawn.

Aggressive Communicators

Aggressive interaction is strong, immediate, obtuse, and controlling. Verbal hostility may incorporate trustworthiness without sympathy, or "ruthless genuineness," which is destructive without being valuable. Aggressive communicators are not generally, however, can be, genuinely overbearing and damaging. passive aggressive interaction is indirect, manipulative, disguised, and truly deceitful.

A passive-aggressive

The communicator may report one feeling, however, show something else through their behaviors and attitudes. Passive aggressive interaction can create turmoil, guilt, and discontent in recipients, as well as incite contempt and a victim complex in speakers. People with narcissistic or borderline personalities are often passive-aggressive communicators.

Assertive

Assertive interaction is straightforward, immediate, mindful, and sure. Self-assured communicators are open and firm, unequivocally grounded in their right to communicate mindfully. Self-assured communicators moderate their trustworthiness with sympathy. They are happy to bargain when appropriate and trust their judgment against control.

Outline: find your communication style

Assertiveness isn't only a interaction style, but a lifestyle.

Self-assured interaction is only one part of demonstrating your right to be treated with kindness and respect. All things considered, how you communicate can significantly affect how individuals view and respond to you.

Which one best describes you?

- Composing exercise: Pick a situation that upsets you. Devise one sentence in response to the incidence using each of the four interaction styles. Be inventive! Evaluate various styles and focus on how you feel practicing in a generally safe manner.

Model: your sibling borrows your vehicle without asking and brings it back without any gas in the tank and an dent on the bumper. How would you address this situation with him?

- I-statements: A key part of confidence is realizing you reserve the right to communicate your wants and needs. Some survivors of psychological abuse battle with being direct in identifying how they feel and requesting what they need. Here, you will work on using clear, direct I-statements to communicate your wants and needs. Keep in mind: asking isn't requesting. Communicating your needs isn't narrow-minded.

- Exercise: Devise an indirect demand or expression you may typically use. Afterward, revise that expression using an immediate I-statement.

- Models: Indirect expression: "It would really be good if you could be a little more pleasant to me."

I-statement: "I want you to be more compassionate towards me," or, "I don't like when you call me names."

Aberrant expression: "When you ridicule my emotions, it makes me feel like you believe I'm absurd for having them."

I-statement: "I have a right to my feelings. You may not agree with them. However, I need you to respect them."

Aberrant expression:

____

____

____

____

I-statement:

____

____

____

____

Aberrant expression:

____

____

____

____

I-statement:

____

____

____

Aberrant expression:

____

____

____

I-statement:

____

____

____

Aberrant expression:

____

____

____

I-statement:

Aberrant expression:

I-statement:

Hindrances to assertiveness

Have you ever at any point asked why you can be confident in certain circumstances, while, others leave you silenced and confounded?

Perhaps you can be assertive for the benefit of your child, but being assertive for yourself gives you hives. Or on the other hand, you can walk straight up to somebody abusing someone else and tell them off, however requesting that your manager approve your vacation time makes your knees shake. What is the contrast between the two situations, where you can be confident in one and in another you can't?

Sometimes we hold unconscious beliefs about ourselves that impact our practices in unpretentious manners. This activity identifies any unconscious beliefs you may have and look at how these beliefs may influence your ability to stand up for yourself. Expound on a time when you were self-confident.

____

____

____

____

What type of thoughts and emotions did you have at that time?

____

____

____

What triggered you to talk or act in that circumstance?

____

____

____

____

Now consider a time when you needed to be self-confident but proved unable. What happened?

____

____

____

____

What type of thoughts and feelings did you have at the time?

____

____

____

What caused you to not stand up for yourself at the time?

____

____

____

What is different about these two situations? How did you communicate with yourself in each situation?

____

____

____

____

De-pleasantify yourself

Raise your hand if your past experiences to stand up for yourself were ever met with some variety of "that is not very reasonable." Niceness has been used—to influence—to overpower and control individual expression by carefully characterizing how and while communicating a need is satisfactory. Individuals of all sexual orientations can be dependent upon solid cultural messages about delightfulness.

Women are socially required to be decent, enchanting, pleasant, sympathetic, adaptable, and obliging. Men are instructed that greatness is a cash for ladies' sexual commitment. Nonetheless sexual orientation desires, minority populaces are regularly unjustifiably troubled by a desire to be decent while standing up to mistreatment or misuse, in case their promotion be considered "excessively forceful.

In these cases, the people are taught to put on a mask—one that disguises their true feelings beneath a layer of "delightfulness." In neither one of the cases can the people be completely reasonable and honest. Delightfulness comes with loss of honesty and legitimacy. This isn't to imply that that the best way to be credible is to act like a jerk. It is to state, however, that it is possible to be thoughtful, empathetic, genuine, and honest without you putting the "need" to be "decent" over your own needs.

What lessons have you received about being decent? Record what you've been instructed.

Model: If I make a misogynist joke at work, individuals will believe I'm a "downer" and a "feminazi." I should simply figure out how to release these situations. (I ought to be tranquil and pleasing—otherwise known as, "decent.")

____

____

____

____

Compose a counter to every one of these messages.

____

____

____

____

Model: If I make a misogynist joke at work, I am defining a limit and communicating my opinion. My thoughts and feelings are important. (I shouldn't bother to suppress my judgement to appease an rude colleague).

____

____

____

____

Fears of a people-pleaser

Withdrawn individuals often fear that self-confidence will appear to be egotistical or aggressive. An obliging person's greatest fear is to upset another person. Be that as it may, what makes that fear so extreme? What might be so awful about upsetting somebody? In this activity, you examine hidden feelings of fear that impact your need to please others. This activity is adapted from techniques used in a restorative model called inner family systems. As you work through this activity, you will see a particular question repeated a few times. Do your best to answer the question each time as a reasonable, non-sarcastic, non-explanatory request. Channel the self-confidence you created in section 3 as you interact with the fearful parts of yourself.

Start by recollecting a time when you needed to stand up for yourself, however, did not out of fear of upsetting someone. Consider how you felt in that second. Why did you experience stress or fear if after upsetting the individual?

I was concerned/anxious that:

____

____

____

____

Listen to the fear. Maybe some part of you is worried about the possibility that if you don't please others, say, doing your mom's bidding, she will be angry with you. Now, with keen attention, ask yourself, "And what would be so bad if that happened?"

What might be the most extremely horrific reaction you've given?

____

____

____

____

Listen again for the fear. Maybe this part is worried about the possibility that if your mom is furious at you, she will think you are an terrible child. With keen attention, ask yourself, "And why would it be bad for me if that happened?"

____

____

____

____

What might be the most extremely terrible reaction you've given?

____

____

Listen once more. Maybe this part of you fears that if your mom thinks you are a bad child, you genuinely will be a bad child. Furthermore, that would be terrible since the most extremely terrible part of being an bad child is that she probably won't love you any longer.

Be considerate, caring, and patient with the parts of you reluctant to cause trouble. Repeating this question, "What would be the most noticeably awful part?" might be likely to get to the deep fear that drives your family satisfying behavior. Keep on offering self-sympathy to your most fearful parts and advise them that you can love and care for yourself regardless of what any other individual does.

Intelligent listening

Intelligent listening alludes to another part of assertive interaction: hearing the other individual's interests. To practice intelligent listening, listen carefully to what the other individual is saying. At that point, when it's your turn to talk, calmly repeat what you heard. Utilize the individual's precise words to show your comprehension of their thoughts or feelings. This sort of listening shows the individual you are concentrating, and you're paying attention to them.

Do this process again.

When you experience gaslighting, for yourself and attempting to persuade the gaslighter that your feelings, thoughts, or memories are important might be appealing. These strategies are typically useless, since the purpose of gaslighting is to persuade you that you are wrong. At times the best system is to the think of a short-expression you can come back to again and again varying—the do this process again.

Do this process again expressions should:

1) recognize the other individual's position, and

2) repeat your response.

Model:

Juan: "You have to stay at home with the children today, so I can go watch the game at Bill's."

Esme: "I realize you need me to stay home today. However, as of now I have plans so you should find a sitter."

Juan: "You are narrow-minded."

Esme: "I realize you need me to stay home today in the evening, but I have plans so you should find a babysitter."

Juan: "I can't trust you. What is wrong with you? How can you be so cold to your own family?"

Esme: "I understand that you're upset, but I previously made arrangements, what's more, I am not dropping them. You should find a sitter. I am leaving now. I'll message when I'm on my way home."

Create three do this process again expressions to confidently stand your ground:

Do this process again #1:

____

____

____

Do this process again #2:

____

____

____

Do this process again #3:

____

____

____

____

Find a workable compromise

Being assertive doesn't mean demanding to get your way all the time. Assertive interaction includes considering and regarding the necessities and concerns everything being equal. Once in a while, the proper conclusion is finding a functional trade-off between two restricting needs. To find a functional trade-off, use logical listening to identify the clashing needs. At that point, make a counter-offer you accept manages equivalent thought to your requirements just as to the necessities of the other individual.

Note: when you are in a severe situation, and your victimizer is attempting to bulldoze you, you must be firm in supporting your wishes. Finding a really functional trade-off surmises a negligible shared respect in a relationship.

This activity encourages you to work on offering a functional trade-off that doesn't cause you to feel bulldozed while recognizing the needs of the other individual.

Models:

"I hear that you truly need to talk with me about this situation. However, I have to complete what I am really going after this moment. We should check in a short ways from now when I can give you my full consideration?"

"I am not ready to dog sit for you this weekend, however, here is the site of a friend of mine who maintains a dog sitting business."

"I'm grieved; however, I can't credit you cash again this month. On any off chance that you might want, I could plunk down with you one week from now and examine your spending plan. Possibly I can assist you with figuring out how to extend your dollars somewhat further."

The request:

____

____

____

____

Your workable compromise:

The request:

Your workable compromise:

The request:

Your workable compromise:

Review and wrap-up. Lookback at the activities in this section.

What impacted you the most?

____

____

____

____

What didn't resonate?

____

____

____

____

How do you feel as of now? Have your feelings changed since you began this part?

____

____

____

____

Establishing Boundaries

Welcome to stage three in your gaslighting recovery. This section provides approaches to establish boundaries in current and future relationships. Learning this skill is a critical part of your recovery, in light of the fact that strong, sound limits are fundamental for relationships to grow and prosper.

This section's activities and arranged instances are intended to help you recognize and set up boundaries that work for you. Starting with an examination of what boundaries are and what they mean to you, it then moves into identifying your own qualities and limits and figuring out how to say "no" without blame.

You may consider establishing boundaries terrifying or awkward. Feeling like this is normal. You have most likely worked hard to abstain from alienating or upsetting your victimizer however much as can be expected.

Resisting the desire of a controlling someone can be a definite way to agitate them. Establishing boundaries doesn't ensure that a victimizer's behavior will improve. Be that as it may, the limits allow you figure out what you will and will not endure, why you will or won't take interest in seeing someone, and where your leave lines are. Boundaries are strengthening.
How about we start.

CHAPTER FIVE

Boundaries defined

Boundaries are what separates one individual, place, or thing from another. You can figure out how to deal with your limits in a wide range of areas, including physical property, physical space/association, mental and romantic commitment, sexual activity, socialization, and time.

Actuality from fiction: separating myths, and, truths about boundaries

What are the truths and myths about boundaries? You may have heard numerous inferences about how boundaries work and whether they are acceptable.

Here, we will dispel a some of the legends you may have experienced, and displace them with realities.

Myth: Establishing limits will make another person change their harmful behavior.

There is a general misinterpretation that boundaries are methods used to change another person's behavior. While that is justifiable, establishing boundaries is about you, not the other individual.

Truth: Establishing boundaries characterizes your actions and decisions. You can't control someone else's behavior. Creating boundaries with the expectation of controlling another person's actions will often incite displeasure. The other individual's response isn't heavily influenced by you. Your behaviors and decisions are.

Myth: Establishing boundaries implies I'm setting up walls to keep others out.

In trapped or harmful relationship, efforts to establish boundaries might be wrongly depicted as dismissal.

Truth: Boundaries are similar to a picket fence, with an gate you can open or on the other hand close.

Setting up sound boundaries isn't a dismissal, but a good decision to associate with someone else. You may decide to unwind your limits for people who exhibit respect, care, compassion, and love for you.

Myth: Establishing limits is heartless, destructive, and mean. You should to never say "no" to somebody you love.

Gaslighters may use a false accusation of cruelty to manipulate you into giving them their way. One strategy for manipulating is to suggest, infer, or downright denying them in any capacity is a cold demonstration.

Truths: Establishing boundaries shows others how to be in a cherishing relationship with you and allows you to be your best self in your relationships.

Cherishing relationships don't include forcing and constraining one another.

When you establish boundaries and stand up for yourself, you show the other individual you respect and care for yourself—and that you expect the same from them. What's more, when you love yourself enough to expect caring, respectful treatment seeing someone, you will sparkle.

What myths do you assume about boundaries? Outline the myths you have assumed, followed by truths to counter them.

Myth:

____

____

____

____

Truth:

____

____

____

____

Myth:

____

____

Truth:

Myth:

Truth:

Myth:

____

____

Truth:

____

____

____

____

Abilities assessment exercise

Boundaries are the lines between two things; however, what creates those lines? Regarding relationship boundaries, you develop the lines by being clear about your own abilities. Characterizing your abilities allows you to know what is and disapproves of you. Limits seeing someone have a double quintessence—where you end and the other individual starts, and what is and is not adequate for you seeing someone. This activity allows you to analyze each type of relationship boundary and express your abilities for every area.

Material boundaries

Material boundaries have to do with your assets—telephones, clothes, money, shoes, cars, electronic gadgets, and so on. You may have limits on what physical property your loan and for to what extent, how your assets are utilized and rewarded, and how to deal with abuse.

Material boundaries might be tested seeing someone where you are expected to give free access to your own property.

Evaluating your values:

Are you happy with crediting out or parting with your material assets? Truly, no, or under what conditions?

____

____

____

____

Are there things you would prefer not to share, loan out, or have lost? How do you feel about saying no?

____

____

____

____

How do you like to communicate your qualities around material belongings?

____

____

____

____

Physical boundaries

Physical boundaries have to do with your body, individual space, and security. How do you feel about individuals being in your physical space, and how would you ensure it? Physical boundaries might be tested in relationships where individuals don't respect your need for individual space or on the other hand protection, or where you have not been allowed to decrease physical contact.

Evaluating your qualities

What level of physical contact would you say you are ok with among friends? Associates? Family? Romantic partners? What level of physical contact feels unacceptable in any of these relationships?

____

____

____

What are your abilities in terms of protection? Do you prefer individuals leave the room before you change clothes? Breastfeed your child? Are you alright with somebody talking with you through the door while you're using the bathroom?

____

____

____

____

How do you like to communicate your qualities around protection?

____

____

____

Mental and emotional boundaries

Mental boundaries allude to having your own considerations and opinions, separate from how another person may think. Emotional boundaries allude to your feelings and emotional responses to situations. These limits might be tested seeing someone where you are relied upon to think and have a feeling that every other person and freedom isn't esteemed.

Assessing your values:
How significant is framing your own thoughts and feelings, regardless of whether these vary from the thoughts and opinions of everyone around you?

____

____

____

____

How significant is having your own feelings, regardless of whether your emotional experiences vary from everyone around you?

____

____

____

____

____

____

How do you actually like to have the option to react when somebody pressures you to think or feel as they do?

____

____

____

____

____

Emotional boundaries can likewise be tested when somebody tries to guilt-trip you into consistence or attempts to make you responsible for their emotional response. How would respond to somebody testing your boundaries along these lines?

____

____

____

____

____

____

____

____

____

____

____

____

____

____

Sexual boundaries have to do with what you are ok with in terms of sexual expression, action, and association. Sexual boundaries additionally envelop romantic contribution, intrigue or absence of interest in sexual contact, and agreement. Your sexual boundaries might be tested by individuals who pressure you into doing things you would prefer not to do, are rude or demanding as sexual partners, or who don't respect your substantial freedom.

Evaluating your values:

How would you express your sexuality? What feels directly for you?

____

____

____

____

____

What expressions of sexuality feel awkward or wrong for you? Such expressions may include sexual acts, explicit type of relationships (e.g., dom/sub relationships, open relationships, monogamous relationships), or a specific sexual orientation (e.g., female/male, sexual orientation assigned during childbirth, hermaphrodite).

____

____

____

____

____

____

____

How would you establish sexual boundaries? How would you want to say "yes" to what you particularly like and "no" to what you don't like?

____

____

____

____

____

____

____

____

Social and social media boundaries

Social boundaries include what you are and are not happy with among friends, just as in your online life. These boundaries may include which exercises you feel significant to join, , you decide to use (or not use) web-based social networking, and how you invest your energy outside of work or school.

Surveying your values:

How significant are relationships and social activities to you? Are you introverted (recuperate from the alone time) or extraverted (gain energy from being around others)?

____

____

____

____

____

____

Are there any social activities you feel great doing? Are there ones that make you awkward?

____

____

____

____

Do you engage in online networking? Assuming this is the main case, how would you control your use (time, stages, content, and so on.)?

____

____

____

____

Time boundaries

Time boundaries include the degree of time you are happy to provide for someone else, a project, employment, or errand. Your choice may include whether to take on a responsibility, selecting to what extent to be included, and when you're finished with something.

Surveying your values:

What is your opinion about offering time to individuals who request or anticipate it?

____

____

____

____

Do you feel good imposing limitations, structure, or boundaries on how you give or utilize your time? Why or why not?

____

____

____

____

____

____

Do you feel like others reserve a right to your time? Assuming this is the case, who?

____

____

____

____

____

Four "yes" or "no" questions.

Before you can choose whether a request fits within your boundaries, you need to know whether the request assists your qualities. Expanding on the "abilities assessment exercise" in this section, take a situation, regardless of whether real or fictional and work through whether the situation fits within your boundaries. Select situations you feel you are likely to experience, or may as of now have experienced, and answer every one of the following questions to explain your "yes" or "no."

What are my abilities in this situation?

Review the manners in which this situation tests, questions, or fits with your individual abilities. Which esteems does this situation support and which does it challenge?

____

____

____

____

Does the activity required in this situation fit my abilities? Activity may include talking, act or declining to act in a specific way. How do these activities or the absence of activities fit with your individual abilities?

How do you feel to be asked to do this? Do you believe you can clearly, effectively, and generously oblige to this demand? Does doing so cause you to feel blameworthy? Angry?

Does saying "yes" or "no" feel, right? Do you have an instinctive response that feels authentic? Do you feel forced to say "yes" when you'd rather say "no"? Do you need more time to consider it?

____

____

____

____

Boundary drawing exercise

This activity encourages you to make a visual representation of your current boundaries, just like a vision of your future. Your current boundaries may be categorized as one of three kinds: powerless, inflexible, or sound. Examine the description below for a visual representation of each type of boundary:

Since people and relationships are complex, your boundaries may be a mixture of the different types. You may have powerless boundaries with your children, however inflexible ones with your life partner. Or on the other hand, you may have powerless boundaries with an associate, however inflexible limits with your family.

Draw an image of the type of limits (or a mixture of types) that you feel most speaks to your current boundaries. You may utilize various types to depict associations with various types of boundaries (for instance, red to represent inflexible boundaries, yellow for powerless boundaries, green for sound), or utilize various images to speak to each type. As you draw, observe how the various relationships and types influence you. What do you notice about your drawing? Next, draw an image of how you'd like your boundaries to be. How does this image differ from the first? What will you have to change to restore your following picture?

Blame messages unmasked
Controllers may show their dissatisfaction with your boundaries by using blame messages. These messages are customized to cause you to believe you have violated the other individual so you will

come back to your past lack of involvement. Blame messages are additionally used to hide the person's actual emotions about your boundaries—regardless of whether that implies outrage, misery, hatred, hurt, or fear. When you perceive the genuine face behind the blame mask, you can ask yourself an important question: is this belief coming from me, or them?

Boundary guilt bingo

Numerous survivors of toxic relationships have a hard time setting boundaries because of serious feelings of blame. They accept the myths and feel that by defining boundaries, they are being egotistical, cruel, or dismissing.

The following is a list of responsible thoughts and feelings that may interfere with your capacity to define boundaries. Report any that resound with you and expound on how these thoughts and feelings influence your capacity to establish boundaries in your relationships. Which of the first statements resonated most for you? Which did not resonate?

____

____

____

____

____

____

____

How has blame made establishing boundaries throughout your life troublesome?

____

____

____

____

Family stories

How did your family feel about boundaries? As you developed through youth, adolescence, and adulthood, did your family support you building up your significant, own point of view? Or on the other hand, were you expected to accept family or parental expectations paying little mind to your own beliefs? Were the standards different for various relatives?

Expound on how your family responded to your efforts—or the efforts of others—to set up boundaries and individuality.

Model 1: Uncle frank was the exemplification of "powerlessness to leave." He lived with granny until she died. He attempted to move in with a girlfriend once. However, the rest of the family made him to feel as though he was forsaking granny, so he stayed.

Model 2: I needed to set off for college to another country. However, my mother cried and said I was making her extremely upset, so I went to junior college, and, I also lived at home. I felt like such an terrible person whenever I even stayed out late since she'd stay up and tell me how stressed she had been the entire time.

____

____

The course of events of your self-improvement

In section 4, you made a course of events of your self-improvement (see "history of growth timeline,"). Here, you make a course of events of your journey to finding your individualism. Starting with your youth, create a visual, demonstrating each progression of establishing, testing, and modifying boundaries through the phases of growth.

Your child years, for instance, will presumably include a great deal of testing of what might occur if you didn't follow directions at home or school. High schooler years may include a greater amount of that, in addition to testing new haircuts, leisure activities and interests, and friend groups. Your adolescence may include choices about advanced education, profession direction, and dating partners.

As you note each formative boundary change, also note how your family reacted. Did your parents motivate four-year-old you to say "No, thank you" when you would not like to embrace a distant family member, or did they state denying an embrace was rude? Did your dad take steps to throw you out of the house for getting a tattoo at 18, or did he motivate you in finding your own type of self-expression?

Boundary wheel

At the point when you are hazy about what your obligations are (and are definitely not), establishing compelling boundaries is hard. At last, boundaries consistently come down to overseeing what is inside your control. In the case, how would you realize what is in your control, and what is another person's to oversee?

Gaslighting obscures the lines. The gaslighter stands to profit by forcing you into assuming responsibility for things that aren't yours. The following outline will assist you in explaining the differences between what you are answerable for, and what you are most certainly not:

What stands out to you about this visual? Where have your boundary lines become obscured? How can you give responsibility back to another person?

____

____

____

____

Mine or not mine

The center of establishing boundaries in any relationship is making an understood limitations among yourself and someone else. Fundamentally, boundaries pose the question, "Is this mine, or not mine?" In this activity, you will inspect a series of vignettes and evaluate whether the introducing issue or then again, concern has a place with you or the other individual.

Care conundrum

Your ex has had her weekend with the children, and she is two hours late bringing them home. You text her asking when she'll be back since the kids have school the following day and she promised to return them by dinnertime. Your ex fires back, blaming you for attempting to cut into her time with the children and trying to control her.

You are angry. However, you try to advise her calmly that the maintenance agreement states what time the children should be home and that you are basically following the agreement. Your ex blames you for her feeling detached from the children, expressing that you put adhering to the rules above family relationships. You feel terrible on the grounds that you know the children miss her, and you're uncertain that you are doing something wrongly by asking her to follow the maintenance agreement.

Who is answerable for the status of your ex's relationship with your children?

Shouldn't it be said that this circumstance isn't your responsibility?

What, if anything, are you answerable for in this circumstance?

____

____

____

Getting a move on

Your supervisor requests that you stay late again today around evening time since one of your group members fell behind in their work, and a project is past due. You don't get additional time when you stay late, and your work was finished in an ideal design. You realize the task is important. However, you detest that your supervisor expects that you should do the work for another person. "If Jerry just did what he should, I wouldn't be having hot pockets for supper for the third night this week," you protest as you settle back in behind your work area. Your partner will be distraught; however, what can you be able to do?

Who is answerable for the delay of the work project?

____

____

____

Shouldn't something be said about this circumstance.
Can it be said that it is someone else's concern?

____

____

____

____

____

What, if anything, are you answerable for in this circumstance?

____

____

____

____

____

Your brother's keeper

Your dad is furious with your younger sibling for disobeying him and getting a tattoo. Your sibling is 20 years of age, yet your dad despite everything expects respect and all-out responsibility. Whenever you don't quickly join your father in disapproving your sibling's choice, he loses control with you also, blames you for urging your sibling to rebel. He says that getting a tattoo is only the first step, and when your sibling winds up poor and on drugs, the fault will lie with you for not keeping him in line. Afterwards, your sibling calls and inquires as to why you didn't advise your dad to chill out. You're presently the trouble maker to the two individuals.

Who is answerable for your sibling's choice to get a tattoo? For your father's response?

____

____

____

____

____

____

How are your boundaries being tested in this circumstance?

What, if anything, are you answerable for in this circumstance?

Who are boundaries for?

Numerous individuals try to establish boundaries in the expectations of making another person stop doing something cruel or upsetting (see "truth from fiction: separating myths and realities about boundaries"). The issue is, we can't control what another person does. Defining limits with the objective of changing another person is setting yourself up for failure.

Boundaries are not so much about the other individual—they are about you, and the space you need in a certain relationship. Boundaries let others understand who you are and what you disapprove of. They characterize where you end, and the other individual starts. They likewise convey what you will do if the other individual disregards your request to stop an upsetting or on the other hand, rude behavior.

Thus, they should essentially be encompassed by "I statements" imparting what you will do in a specific circumstance (review the "I-statements" topic in section 4).

For instance, "I think that it's rude when you make remarks about my weight. If you continue doing so, I will end the discussion." This immediate statement shows how the other individual has crossed a line (making unwanted and more, hurtful remarks), how these words influence you (hurt emotions), and how you will react if the other individual does not respect your request to stop (finishing the discussion).

Standard procedures for establishing boundaries

Although being centered around your own interest in a relationship, boundaries should follow a couple of general rules to be convincing. Here are four essential guidelines for setting up boundaries:

1. Express clear definitions.

Plainly express the issue. Making unclear, overgeneralized statements like "you're mean" isn't useful. Recognize the risky behavior by name. "Making savage jokes to my disadvantage is mean" characterizes the hurtful behavior all the more clearly.

2. Be explicit.

"You generally do this/you never do that" is extremely broad and doesn't really communicate the extent of the issue. Inclining to explicit behaviors, situations, or requests strengthens your position. "You punched the door directly before me and afterwards denied hitting it."

3. Use I-explanations.

Keep in mind, boundaries are about you and characterize your space. Use I-explanations to indicate how hurtful behaviors intrudes on your space, regardless of whether genuinely, intellectually, inwardly, or in other ways. "When you kept on agitating me after I requested that you stop; I felt furious and affronted. If you agitate me once more, I'll get up and leave."

4. Set practical outcomes.
Establishing boundaries include setting outcomes if what you've established is overlooked. What will you do if somebody doesn't respect

the boundary you set? Be ready with a result you can consistently continue. Rather than saying, "If you talk to me that way, I'll never address you again," try, "In the event that you misgender me again after I've asked you not to, I will leave."

Levels of contact
As much as we would wish in any case, some will be reluctant to respect or respond to your boundaries, regardless of how assertive you are, or how practical your boundaries may be. In these relationships, you may consider obliging the potential for hurt by pulling

back to a lower level of interaction with that individual.

Using low-contact lessens the potential for progressing abuse.
By restricting how much time you spend with a victimizer. In a low-contact relationship, you may avoid generally social efforts but remain slightly associated through periodic calls, messages, or instant messages. Low contact might be a great alternative for family members, ex-life partners with whom you should co-parent, and partners whom you can't completely maintain a strategic distance from.

No contact takes low-contact to its endpoint: cutting off a relationships. You don't connect with the other individual, and you don't respond to their efforts. You may completely stay away from settings where you may see them. In extreme cases, you may move to an different city or state to escape from the individual. No contact is commonly saved for instances of serious, continuous, and unapologetic abuse.

Ten ways to say "no" (that aren't mean)

Numerous individuals battle with saying "no" in light of the fact that they have a feeling that they are mean, egotistical, or unfeeling. Actually, there is not all that much about defining a boundary. Ensuring your time, energy, and space allows you to connect all the more energetically and benevolently during a certain time based on your personal preference.

An assertive "no" is preferable to a hesitant "yes."

Here are ten different ways to say "no" that is not mean:

1. No.
2. That doesn't work for me.
3. Apologies, I can't do that.
4. I can't do this thing, but I can do that other thing.
5. That doesn't feel right to me.
6. I'm not alright with that.

7. Perhaps some other time.

8. I appreciate you asking; however, I have to say "no."

9. No, bless your heart.

10. I'd prefer not to.

Would you be able to consider different approaches to saying "no"? Outline with some choices here.

____

____

____

____

____

____

____

____

Managing   pushback: flying monkeys

Flying monkeys are named after the animals that take care of the wicked witch of the west in the "Wizard of Oz". In the film, the witch sends her animals to harass and catch Dorothy, assigning them to do her dirty work for her. Using someone, flying monkeys fill in as go-betweens, attempting to bring recently free friends or relatives once more into the fold.

Flying monkeys regularly join for the benefit or at the command of the gaslighter. They draw on the victim's feelings and inner pain for a more beneficial relationship. Flying monkeys may pressure, humiliate, control, or coax victims to bring them back under the influence of the victimizer. While flying monkeys may see themselves as peacemakers or middle people, they are typically taking a shot at the benefit of the controller—the gaslighter who wouldn't like to release their victim.

Example: Amari felt heartbroken defining boundaries with her mother. However, she was unable to take the detached forceful remarks, hidden responses and castigating any longer. This would be the first Christmas she didn't spend with her mother. Despite the fact that she knew her choice not to go was right, she was deeply saddened.

A couple of days before Christmas, Amari got a call from her auntie, asking if she was going back home for Christmas. When Amari made it clear that she required some space from her mother, her auntie reprimanded her for refusing her mom by disrespecting her on Christmas. Amari hung up the telephone and cried. The following day, she got another call—this time from her grandma. "Amari," her mother's mother stated, "Your mom isn't great, but you are taking this too far. Go back home and work it out with her." The calls and messages from family members continued until the day before Christmas. However, Amari's mom never called her.

Amari experienced flying monkeys as her auntie, grandma, and other family members.

Have you experienced flying monkeys in your relationships? Write about your experience(s) here.

Managing pushback, part 2: get-in-line messages

Get-in-line messages are unpretentious or palpable messages to get you to come back to your usual place inside the gaslighter's authoritative reach. Flying monkeys may use get-in-line messages if appealing to your feelings doesn't work. These messages are an effort to humiliate you into agreeing.

Example: Jacob had been close to his dad as a child; however, their relationship became strained because of his dad's substance abuse. He excused his dad's drunk driving and other dangerous decisions numerous times; however, in the end, decided he was unable to continue. Whenever his father got into an accident because of driving drunk, Jacob did not come to help. His dad called Jacob's younger sibling,

Seth, who drove out to haul their dad's vehicle out of a dump.

Jacob was found napping when Seth showed up to his home after 12 pm that night, seething. "How can you leave me to manage dad what's more, you simply stay here on your couch sitting in front of the tv?" he requested. "I just spent hours getting his vehicle out of the dump and making sure he didn't have a blackout, and you can't be bothered to help? How egotistical are you? I can't believe you wouldn't support your own family." Jacob reminded Seth he had played out these very actions for a considerable length of time without grumbling. However, Seth couldn't have cared less. "You don't get the opportunity to leave family," he said indignantly. "If this situation happens once more, you better come and help, or the entire family will realize what type of person you truly are." Seth humiliated Jacob and blamed him for childishness trying to pressure him into his old job as family empowering influence and problem solver.

Have you experienced get-in-line messages in your relationships? Write about your experience(s) here.

Perceiving the subtle signs

At the point when you have experienced childhood in or invested a great deal of energy in helpless boundaries, observing when your boundaries have been disrespected can be troublesome. Doing so isn't generally as evident as drawing a line in the sand and advising somebody not to make a step, at that point observing them tap move over the line with a "so what?"

Focusing on the unobtrusive signs can help enlighten you to when your boundaries are in being unwittingly tested. Consider a time when something felt awkward, by one way or another wrong, or outright off. You may have had a suspicion that something wasn't right, however very little clarity on what precisely wasn't right. Look at that the memory with the following questions.

Questions:

What feelings did I have in that circumstance?

____

____

____

What thoughts did I have in that circumstance?

____

____

____

What physical feelings did I have in that circumstance?

____

____

____

Boundary stomping

Boundary steps are definitely not unobtrusive. A boundary step happens when somebody interprets your establishment of a boundary as an individual attack. Boundary stompers accept their requests and want to override all others. They will see the lines you set up as a test and may toe that line usually before stepping over the line and inciting a response. The gaslighter may then utilize your response to gaslight you, especially if they describe the response as ridiculous.

Some examples of boundary stepping include:

• the relative who overlooks your guidelines about how to feed your baby, giving her frozen yoghurt after you disclose to her the child is not ready to start solid foods.

• the boyfriend who demands to order for you at cafés, in spite of the fact that he generally chooses fish knowing you despise it. He is certain you will come to adore the fish as much as he does if you (are compelled to) eat it enough.

• the friend who borrows your vehicle and changes all your preset radio broadcasts or signs you up for a satellite radio program membership using your money.

• the manager who over and again expects that you should deal with work issues on your days off, messaging or calling you continually until you stop what you were doing to take care of the issue.

How have you experienced limit stepping in your life?

____

____

____

How did you react to it?

____

____

____

Connect with, disengage, or make a strategic retreat

Finally, not many activities have examined various ways individuals throughout your life may neglect to respect the limits you set. This activity presents three alternatives for responding when your limits are disrespected or overlooked. At the point when somebody challenges your boundaries, you have three essential decisions: connect, separate, or make a key retreat.

Connect with: sometimes you may decide to address the other individual in the moment. You may bring up how they are crossing a line, clarify why respecting what you've laid out is important, or help them to remember the outcomes in the event that they don't stop what they're doing. If they contend or question why it makes a difference, you may clarify or essentially emphasize your position (review the "do this process again" responses you made in part 4).

Imagine a circumstance where your boundaries are crossed, and you'd prefer to connect.

____

____

____

____

Separate: there will be times when somebody challenges a boundary and, you know nothing will be solved by talking about the situation. You can withdraw from impasse discussions by hanging up the telephone, leaving, not answering to an instant message, or changing the subject.

At the point when a gaslighter attempts to trap you by testing your feeling of situations, you may withdraw by expressing, "We recollect what occurred in an unexpected way. There doesn't actually appear to be a need to keep talking about this issue."

Think about a circumstance where you would want to withdraw.

____

____

____

____

Key retreat: when you realize you will enter a situation where gaslighting, flying monkeys, boundary stepping, or get-in-line messages are probably going to happen, consider leaving yourself space for a key retreat. Park your vehicle toward the exit or remain close to a door, so you have the choice of leaving. If a difference is heightening and you feel unsafe, you are not committed to remain and proceed to be abused.

Think about a circumstance where you may require a key retreat.

____

____

____

Expanding on your history

There is a first time opportunity for everything, including defining boundaries. Think about your past efforts to set up boundaries with someone.

Regardless of whether you don't think, you worked superbly, or in the event that they appeared useless, those early efforts are the seeds of figuring out how to have space for yourself.

What type of boundaries have you attempted to set previously?

____

____

____

What worked out positively in your past efforts?

____

____

____

What went poorly?

____

____

____

What can you do now?

____

____

____

What did you find out about yourself and the other individual in this circumstance?

____

____

____

What boundaries would you like to set in your life now?

____

____

____

What can you be able to do currently, knowing what you do?

____

____

____

Consent to leave/permission to stay

At the point when abuse is continuous, and the odds of anything changing are slim to none, you can make your key retreat a lasting one. Despite the fact that society has numerous ideas about family, responsibility, and friends, your wellbeing and prosperity are important. The choice can be troublesome and deeply painful. However, some relationships can't be rescued.

What needs to happen for you to cut off a relationship? Where is your line in the sand? What do you have to say to yourself to feel like you can leave a harmful or toxic relationship?

My line in the sand is:

____

____

____

____

I allow myself to leave in light of the fact that:

____

____

You may have relationships from which you feel unable or unwilling to leave. In the event that you decide to stay, consider what you need that relationship to look like with the goal for you to be comfortable. How might you make your situation the ideal situation?

My motivations to stay:

____

____

____

I allow myself to:

____

____

____

Defensive visualization

There might be times when you can't refrain from investing energy into someone who challenges your wholehearted and mental boundaries. For those times, this experience can assist you with remembering that you don't have to accept their attack into your space. You may play out this concise reflection previously, you see the boundary pusher, or when you sense them testing your boundaries at the time.

Start by getting mindful of the physical boundary of your skin.

Notice how there's a reasonable line between where your body starts and stops in space. Presently envision a reasonable, adaptable, however solid covering your skin. The covering is permeable, permitting air and positive energy to stream through to you, however opposing negative energy.

Next imagine an unique space or curve tumbling over the boundary pusher. The vault is fixed, keeping them from leaving their own space and entering yours. Their negative energy, gaslighting, manipulating, and other controls are totally held inside the vault with them. In spite of the main fact that they may try to get through the arch and attack your boundaries, your imperceptible covering safeguards you.

At last, they are left inside the arch with whatever energy they have they carried with them.

Confirming your space

Make five statements or mantras that help your right to use and hold space, establish boundaries, and be your own individual.

Say what you look for into reality. Offer appreciation to the universe, or whatever resonates for you deeply, for supporting your boundaries.

Models:

"I have the right to establish boundaries that serve me in my life."

"Consistently I become more clear and more clear about the limits I

want and need."

"I can, without much of a stretch, convey my boundaries and have them respected."

Your turn:

____

____

____

____

Review and wrap-up. Look back at the activities in this section.

What impacted you the most?

____

____

____

____

What didn't resonate?

____

____

____

____

How do you feel now? Have your emotions changed since you began This section?

Recuperating from trauma

A definitive objective of recuperating from gaslighting is to mend the injuries you received in a damaging relationship. As you have worked through the initial two sections, you have created an understanding of how you have been harmed by gaslighting, how your pain has influenced you in relationships, and how to shield yourself from further abuse. Now you direct your focus toward the parts in you that are prepared to recover.

CHAPTER SIX

Self-Care

Well As you move into the last period of this activity guide, pause for a minute to salute yourself for the difficult work you've done up to this point.

You have figured out how to distinguish gaslighting by definition, just as by its signs, manifestations, and effects. You have examined the influence gaslighting has had on you and started to recover by creating self-compassion, self-confidence, and restoring your self-esteem.

The journey from victim to survivor can be an uneven one. You have the right to feel pleased with yourself for each succession of that journey.

In this part, you will establish a self-care routine to help your development and recovery. Various activities here are intended to support you. Explain your self-care needs, recognize hindrances to self-care, and develop a more advantageous way of life.

Keep in mind, addressing your own needs isn't narrow-minded. Dealing with yourself along these lines is, truth be told, significant to being an complete and strong individual. Realizing that you can accomplish something and realizing how to do it, in any case, are two different things. That is the reason for this section: to give you new pieces of knowledge, new thoughts, and new alternatives for dealing with you.

How about we start!

Domains of self-care

Self-care includes five fundamental domains: physical, mental, emotional, religious, and social.

Physical self-care alludes to thinking about your physical body. This kind of care incorporates getting satisfactory rest, eating nutritious food, drinking enough water, getting enough exercise, treating disease or injuries, and taking part in positive affect.

Mental self-care alludes to thinking about your mind. This kind of care incorporates learning new things, testing and changing harmful thought designs, creating cognitive appraisals, resting from mental work, for example, work, and thinking carefully in manners you appreciate.

Emotional self-care alludes to thinking about your heart. This sort of care incorporates interfacing with and approving your feelings, recovering emotional wounds, communicating your emotions carefully, and doing things that make your heart full.

Otherworldly self-care alludes to thinking about your soul. This sort of care may, yet doesn't need to, incorporate strict beliefs and practices.

Otherworldly self-care incorporates contemplation, care, setting goals, insistences, and practicing appreciation.

Social self-care alludes to thinking about yourself inside relationships. This sort of care incorporates settling on choices about whom you invest energy with, having individuality inside a relationship, sustaining romantic relationships, and cutting off or changing destructive friendships.

You may see the cover in a few of these domains. Individuals are mind-boggling and multifaceted; on the grounds that these domains affect each other, thinking about yourself in one domain can have a far-reaching influence of positive energy into another. For instance, scouring a scented salve onto your skin may cause your skin to feel delicate, while likewise inspiring lovely recollections related with the aroma, causing you to feel cheerful and satisfied.

Reading an extraordinary book may open your mind to new ideas, take you through a scope of emotional experiences, and give you something to talk about at your next party.

This activity causes you to create an essential domain of self-care for a number of exercises you recognize—but don't stress if your activities address various domains as this simple method you're getting more for your self-care buck!

Record your five most loved types of self-care right now. What domain(s) do your top picks fall into? Are there any domains you're presently dismissing?

____

____

____

____

Self-care is more

Well to be extremely worthwhile, self-care should be more than sitting down on the sofa and gorging on Netflix all weekend. The intermittent lazy day can be fun, but it's definitely not enough without anyone else to help you with revitalizing and reset. As you start setting up your self-care schedule, keep the following values as the main priority. Self-care is:

Associated: at its center, self-care is tied in with interfacing with your own requirements, needs, and prosperity. If your self-care doesn't cause you to feel more in line with yourself, some alteration might be required.

Dynamic: self-care is in a perfect world a proactive procedure—a piece of your day by day life, as opposed to something you swear by when you're now worn out. Search for little approaches to effectively think about yourself every day, as opposed to holding up until you feel overpowered and depleted.

Reviving: self-care ought to be something that reestablishes the energy you spend on everything else. Regardless of whether your strategy for self-care leaves you truly drained, you ought to feel revitalized in the soul.

Extensive: self-care will develop and extend with you. As a dynamic, developing procedure, your self-care will change as you develop and create. If your typical techniques for self-care are leaving you exhausted, worn-out, or unchanged, it's an ideal opportunity to attempt something new.

Physical self-care: rest, recover, and refresh
If you request an irregular examining from individuals how they practice self-care, a sizable share would almost certainly name resting as one of their top picks.
Work, school, work out, side interests, family commitments, social commitment, online life posts, housework, driving time, staying aware of the news. At whatever day, you may be immersed with chaos and movement from the second your eyes open in the first part of the day until they close in rest around evening time. As a general public, we are progressively occupied, progressively on edge, and progressively tired.
Little wonder, at that point that such a large number of us ache for rest! Furthermore, rest is a significant factor in practicing physical self-care. Getting enough rest allows us to truly recoup from our day, reestablish the energy exhausted by our comings and

goings, and feel revived. Utilize the following questions to measure whether you are getting enough rest:

How much rest do you need every night to feel genuinely refreshed and prepared to get up to begin the next day?

____

____

____

____

How much rest do you really get?

____

____

____

____

In the event that you are not getting enough, what interferes with your rest?

____

____

____

____

Name one social change you can actualize promptly to improve your rest (e.g., no screens for at least an hour before bed, utilize a blue light channel if you do have screens, no caffeine past 1 p.m., and so on.).

____

____

____

____

Rest doesn't just mean sleeping. Getting some much-needed rest to recover from an illness or on the other hand injury, sitting in a thoughtful posture, and meditating to relax gradually and deeply are all methods of resting your body. Name three different ways you can rest.

____

____

____

____

Physical self-care: get moving

On the opposite side of the coin, your body was made to move. Whatever your degree of physicality, physical capacity/portability, or limitations, discovering methods to move your body can be a method for self-care. In any event, for those with physical disabilities and continual pain conditions, for example, fibromyalgia, combining some growth into every day can improve side effects essentially.

Utilize the following questions to examine your physical self-care:

What sorts of physical exercises do you appreciate? The action doesn't need to mean conventional exercise. Anything that gets you moving and feels better will do.

____

____

____

____

How regularly do you take part in these exercises?

____

____

____

If you don't take part in them all the time, what stops you?

____

____

____

____

Name one social change you can execute quickly to increase your physical activity by 10%:

____

____

____

____

Now and again, individuals are reluctant to participate in physical exercises they find challenging. Be that as it may, seeking after a challenge can be energizing and empowering, regardless of whether hard! Identify one physical movement you find testing or on the other hand, somewhat unnerving, and make an arrangement to attempt that movement at any rate once in a month from now.

Example: I will go to the following fledgeling's stone climbing class in my neighborhood climbing exercise center, this Friday at 6 p.m. I will pack my workout clothes and leave them in the vehicle so that I can go directly after work.

____

____

____

Mental self-care: take a break

You've presumably heard (and utilized) the expression "daydreaming" to portray the practice of taking a psychological break. Daydreaming is a substantial alternative for creating good mental behaviors from an issue. However, there are other ways to accomplish this. Utilize the following questions to examine other approaches to take a psychological break:

What type of assignments or circumstances do you find mentally draining?

____

____

____

When do you sense that you need a psychological break? When do you become most mentally drained?

____

____

____

When do your thoughts flee with you?

Example: I can't stop going through my plan for the day around nightfall to observe what I missed.

____

____

____

Name one approach to offer yourself a psychological reprieve without totally daydreaming.

Example: When my mind begins racing, I will compose my thoughts on a notepad I keep by the bed with the goal that I don't need to monitor everything in my head.

____

____

____

Mental self-care: go deeper
Some of the time, mental self-care implies doing something contrary to daydreaming:
Listening and going further. Reading self-improvement guides (like this one!), learning another skill or creating a current one, journaling, and taking part in conscious discussion are generally methods of extending your reasoning.

What's more, appealing your mind in refreshing, fascinating assignments is a type of mental self-care.

Utilize the following questions to investigate how you can connect with, widen, what's more, expand your psyche:

What sorts of exercises, prompts, activities, or questions intrigue you?

What do you find intellectually animating?

____

____

____

What areas do you feel educated about? What might you want to become familiar with?

____

____

____

What is one question (absurd or genuine) you've for a long while been itching to have answered? Look into the appropriate response and quickly work out your response here:

Question:

____

____

____

Answer:

____

____

____

Name one ability you might want to learn, expand, or develop. Identify an asset to start discovering this ability.

Model: I need to figure out how to play the guitar. I will find a YouTube video, what's more, learn one song this week.

____

____

Self-care is not actually selfish

Survivors of psychological abuse sometimes stress that taking time to take care for their own needs implies they are narrow-minded. Has this concern at any point prevented you from dealing with yourself? Assuming this is the case, cheer up. Practicing self-care doesn't mean you are overlooking or stomping on the needs of others for your own advantage. Dealing with yourself is crucial to being present and affectionately engaged in your relationships.

Enthusiastic self-care: acknowledge, validate, what's more, befriend
One of the main losses in a gaslighting relationship is your opportunity of emotional expression. Gaslighters question, condemn and negate your emotions to keep you misled. Your capacity to think about your emotional wellbeing suffers a shot when you are continually told your feelings aren't right. Enthusiastic self-care includes unlearning that message and

supplanting what you've been over and again told with inside approval.

At the point when you have an emotional reaction, delay and notice what you are feeling. Name the emotion(s) here.

Example: I am truly disturbed in the wake of battling with my sweetheart. I am irate, tragic, and humiliated.

____

____

____

At the point when you notice yourself having no feelings, be interested in what is occurring. What are you not allowing yourself to feel?

Example: I go blank when my sweetheart criticizes me. It's better not to feel anything than to be harmed and angry.

____

____

____

Approve your enthusiastic experience, paying little heed to what that experience is.

Example: I am feeling extremely angry at this moment, and my anger is substantial.

____

____

____

Become friends with your emotions. They are informing you concerning how you experience a relationship.

Model: I value my anger since it shows me when somebody is crossing my boundaries. Much obliged to you, anger.

____

____

____

Enthusiastic self-care: heal and discharge

Identifying, approving, and become a close friend with your feelings is a significant part of enthusiastic self-care. Moreover, naming and claiming your feelings is an incredible demonstration of self-esteem that checks the self-erasing messages of gaslighting. In any case, we can get stuck in upsetting emotions and increase the suffering, putting off recovering. Feelings of vulnerability, perceptiveness, disdain, and misery can make moving ahead in your life hard. Here is the where freeing comes in.

Note: Healing and freeing yourself is a procedure. You may need to repeat this practice a few times to feel a discharge. Recovering and freeing yourself from suffering are likewise, perfect objectives with which to start psychotherapy. Try not to be hesitant to start your work here and proceed with a recovery expert.

Recuperating and releasing meditation

Place yourself in an agreeable position, either sitting or standing. Close your eyes and bring forward your inner thoughts . Notice your breathing and pause for a minute to just follow your breath moving all through your body. Notice if your breath feels smooth, open, and free, or forced, fast, and shallow. Stay with your breath until it feels smooth and simple.

Carry your attention to your heart. Welcome the light at the focal point of your being to fill your heart. Feel both the light and your breath as they fill, travel through, and enlighten your heart space. Feel your heart extend with all the adoration, light, and self-compassion it can hold.

Welcome the parts of you that haves suffering to step into the light around your heart. As each injured part enters the light, welcome it. With each breath and with each beat of your heart, send your injured parts love and light. Welcome those injured parts to rest in your heart space for as long as they wish. Allow them to impart to you any accounts, beliefs, or recollections of the injuries they may convey.

At the point when it feels right, welcome your injured parts to free any shame, fault, anguish, or outrage, they feel about their injuring, if they are willing.

If they are not willing, that is alright. They don't have to do anything until they feel prepared.

In the event that an injured party wishes to free themselves of something, this part may send that suffering away from itself in the manner it feels best. Use up or mask the suffering, scatter it to the wind, shoot it into the core of the sun—whatever feels best for that part of you, in the space where the injured part held that suffering welcome in the adoration and light of your heart.

As your heart recovers, its ability for love, light, and self-sympathy will develop. Thank your heart for its boundless limit with regards to recovering. Finish this reflection by sitting in gratitude.

Deep self-care: connect and take in

Deep self-care involves watching out for the needs of your soul. Deep care may, however, don't need to, incorporate strict practices or supplications.

Keeping an eye on the soul may incorporate reflection, thought, or setting goals for yourself. Appreciation, care, and confirmations are all.

Types of profound self-care.

For this activity, you will concentrate on connecting with situations that mitigate your soul. Locate a physical area that conjures feelings of congruence, connection, and positive energy. For some, this area will have a plenitude of nature—someplace like a recreation center, park, forest, or calm seashore. You may sit, stand, rest, or walk.

- Associate and take in

Start by concentrating on what your five senses tell you concerning your condition. Notice the hints of the breeze, your strides on the ground, the temperature and fragrance of the air. Take a taste of water and concentrate the entirety of your thoughts on the vibe of the water, tongue, and throat.

As you walk, feel yourself being a part of nature. Feel associated with the earth through your feet. Feel your head brush the sky. Feel your body travel through the air. Lean into your connection with the world.

Tune in to the elements of your section—your strides crunching on leaves, rock, or sand; your arms as they brush past shrubberies or rub against your sides; your breath as it enters and leaves your body. Hear how your reality adds to the elements of life on the planet.

Find an good spot to sit or lie on the ground. Feel the sun on your body. Feel gravity holding you to the earth. Hear the unobtrusive developments of bugs in the dirt, and the removed beat of birds' wings in the breeze. Hear the buzz of the honey bees and prattling of squirrels. Take in the string of energy that interfaces you to the system of living, breathing creatures. Welcome your connection with nature.

- Otherworldly self-care: brush it off

Otherworldly self-care additionally incorporates freeing and liberating yourself of energy that channels or damages your soul. In the past exercise, you invited and, opened up to nature, feeling your connection with the world. In this activity, you will free yourself of what doesn't serve your soul.

Sit or stand with your back straight and head high.

Imagine the energy of negative beliefs, negative self-talk, and negative experiences as dark rings contacting your skin. Now imagine your heart light developing from inside, squeezing through your skin and breaking the contact with those rings. Inhale deeply as your heart light moves through you, releasing the ringlets and filling you with adoration and light.

Lay your right hand on your left shoulder, and with a firm, invigorated movement, run your hand down your arm. Brush the rings away, proceeding with the movement down your arms and off the ends of your fingertips. Set the goal to get over the negative energy that channels your soul. Repeat the brushing movement as many times as you need until you feel free from the negative energy around your left arm. If find the brushing movement truly difficult, imagine this activity.

Repeat the brushing movement, this time utilizing your left hand to brush off your right arm. Brush the two arms down your upper and lower legs, down your body, and from the top of your head to your shoulders.

- Constantly hold the goal of discharging negative vitality.

Now take in a moderate, full breath through your nose, extending your chest and belly as they fill up with air. With a short, sharp, exhalation, free your breath and utilize your stomach to push some circulation in through your mouth strongly.

Utilize your hands to accentuate the movement of driving air away from you. Structure a slight withdrawal in your midsection as you breathe out. Repeat the inward breath and exhalation until you feel clear and open inside. If you become discombobulated, hold your breath for a couple of minutes while breathing in and breathing out. Finish this activity by sitting or standing tall and firm, breathing ordinarily, and imagine yourself filled up with heart light.

- Social self-care: deepen and nurture

Social self-care alludes to how you deal with yourself inside relationships. One significant part of social self-care is contributing in, sustaining, and developing relationships that feed you. Consider the individuals throughout your life who cause you to feel cherished, supported, and accepted. How might you increment your association with these individuals?

Name at least three individuals who support, love, and accept you.

____

____

____

How do these relationships support you?

What amount of time do you go through with individuals who support you? How would you engage with these supporting relationships?

Identify one way to support these caring relationships consistently.

Thank your friends and family for supporting you with their adoration, support, and acceptance. How might you express your appreciation?

Social self-care: detach and disengage

Some relationships don't support you. Social self-care incorporates separating yourself, from those relationships that channel or hurt you. All relationships carry suffering somewhat, as a struggle, difference, missteps, and hurt are, for the most part, ordinary to some level. Be that as it may, harmful or on the other hand damaging relationships are leaned toward these destructive efforts. How might you limit your presence in such relationships that injury you?

Which relationships throughout your life present to you the most suffering? Identify at least one relationship that is harmful, damaging, or negative.

____

____

____

____

How does this relationship hurt you?

____

____

What amount of time do you go through with individuals who hurt you? What amount do you need to engage with these relationships?

____

____

Identify ways you need to separate or withdraw from toxic partnerships, relationships, and situations. When would you be able to leave, decline a greeting, or leave an relationship?

____

____

Self-care is necessary for healing

The most harming, waiting for the impact of psychological abuse, is the manner in which it detaches you from your feeling of self. Gaslighting detaches you from what contends you in your life: you. Self-care is an important development in your recovery and recuperation process that allows you to reconnect with yourself in a adoring, humane, and approving way.

Practicing self-care reaffirms you that your needs are legitimate, your needs are adequate, and you are deserving of adoration and, consideration.

Contemplative person/extravert

Self-preoccupation and extraversion allude to the manner in which an individual reacts to a social commitment with others. Self-observers discover social commitment tiring and, revive their batteries by investing energy alone. They frequently like little gatherings or one-on-one contribution when they mingle. Extraverts discover socialization stimulating and revive their batteries by spending time with others. They regularly appreciate being in the activity, with a lot of individuals with whom they can talk and lock-in.

Contingent upon whether you are increasingly introverted or extraverted, your self-care needs may look somewhat different. Introverted people will, in general, organize self-care that doesn't expect them to be around others so much.

Extraverts might be less energized to self-care if it doesn't include other individuals. Take the test underneath to discover which side you fall on, and plan your self-care as needs be. For every statement, feature "me" if the explanation concerns you and "not me" if the statement doesn't speak to you.

1. I am frequently seen as social and active.

2. I am frequently seen as reserved and thoughtful.

3. I appreciate being among and working in groups.

4. I lean toward being around one or two individuals. Gatherings make me awkward.

5. I dislike being distant from everyone else.

6. I value my alone time and appreciate my self- talk.

7. I have a big group of friends and colleagues.

8. I know a couple of individuals well overall.

9. I can bounce rapidly into another action or intrigue, in some cases, at the cost of thinking things completely through.

10. I, in some cases, overthink new experiences and may move too slowly.

11. I, in some cases, neglect to stop and consider what I need and what I am trying to accomplish before beginning another task.

12. Some of the time, I neglect to check whether my thoughts and internal experience fit with the outside world.

If you addressed "me" on at least four of the questions, you scored higher on extraversion than introversion. Outline self-care exercises that include being around individuals. If "me" on at least four of the questions, you scored higher on introversion. Your self-care will be increasingly centered around time with yourself or then again not many close friends. In the event that your answers are uniformly part between both, you might be an ambivert—which means you draw equal or fulfilment from exercises fit for introverts or extraverts.

Structure your self-care routine to draw from the two sides.

Full focus

In some capacity, you are now rehearsing a specific measure of day by day self-care.

You take care of and dress, rest around evening time, invest energy with partners, friends and family, and make the most of your preferred leisure activities and interests.

At the point when self-care gets normal, we stop seeing its belongings on our state of mind. This activity will help you carefully pull together on your day by day self-care.

Pick a movement of everyday self-care, for example, eating dinner, taking a shower, or putting on your nightwear. Concentrate your complete consideration on what you are doing. Utilizing whatever number of your abilities as can be allowed, watch each detail you can about the movement as you work through it. Note your state of mind prior to participating in this action, just as during and a short time later. What do you notice?

Self-care action:

____

____

____

State of mind before beginning:

____

____

____

Perceptions utilizing all senses:

____

____

____

Restraints you notice:

____

____

____

State of mind after finishing:

____

____

____

Hoist the mundane

Pick an everyday self-care action to make unique. In the event that you typically take a five-minute shower without any ornaments, give yourself an additional ten minutes to remain under the high temp water and unwind. In the event that you typically scarf down lunch while sending work messages, turn off your telephone or pc and have lunch in a calm, lovely space. Bring careful consideration to what you regularly manage without speculation, and make your everyday self-care a minimal more and more exceptional.

Ten ideas for self-care activities

Now it's your chance to make a situation that supports you in thinking about yourself. Try to give some consideration each day to every one of the five domains—physical, mental, emotional, otherworldly, and social. Still not certain what self-care looks like? Here are ten thoughts to kick you off:

• snuggle a pet. Pets are useful for your wellbeing—mental, emotional, and physical!

• call or get together with a companion. Invest your energy with individuals who love and support you;
• complete one little family task you've been putting off. Calm pressure and accomplish fulfilment by removing something off your plan for the day.

• get outside in the daylight. Daylight is useful for the soul—and a large portion of us can utilize somewhat more vitamin d.

• do your preferred recreation action, for example, a jigsaw puzzle, craftsmanship activity, playing an instrument, or tuning in to music. Having a ton of fun is a demonstration of self-care.

• try another exercise or class. You may find another most loved interest!

• dance. You needn't bother with preparing to move your body. Put on your main tunes and rock out!

• read a book for the sake of entertainment. An extraordinary book can take you anyplace you need to go.

• redecorate or revamp a side of your living space. Make your space a sanctuary.

• go on an experience. Leave, go kayaking, explore another city, or drive someplace only for going.

Review and wrap-up . Look back at the activities in this section.
What impacted you the most?

____

____

____

What didn't resonate?

____

____

____

How do you feel now? Have your feelings changed since you began this action?

____

____

____

What will you detract from these activities?

____

____

____

CHAPTER SEVEN

Setting Up Healthy Connections

In the course of the last six parts, you have analyzed—in extreme detail— what your undesirable relationships resemble. Presently you expand upon all that you've learned to make a more beneficial future. Part 7 has activities and examples intended to assist you with building up a more clear image of the sound relationships you need to develop pushing ahead.

Understanding what has befallen you and how it happened is a significant first phase in recouping from injury and abuse. Be that as it may, this recuperation doesn't stop at understanding past experiences. Recuperation happens when you can take what you think about yourself and your relationships and utilize that understanding to make a more advantageous future.

How about we start.

Finishing the picture

The most intriguing work of art coordinates our concentrate someplace surprising. We may begin taking a look at one part of a charming picture, just to discover our look attracted to a totally extraordinary part inside the piece. Allowing our look to be drawn away from the quick or clear zone of focus allows us to see an increasingly complete, point by point, and nuanced picture.

As we start investigating the relationships we wish to transform, we can become extremely centered around the undesirable relationships that made us initially start looking at this image. Identifying undesirable circumstances is a significant skill, be that as it may, if we stop at just identifying our toxic relationships, we miss another significant component of the master plan: the emergence of a sound relationship. Similarly, as with artistry, we get a progressively complete picture by figuring out how to perceive what wasn't quickly in focus upon first look.

This activity allows you to start examining what a sound relationship looks like by distinguishing attributes that are contrary to the harmful and ruinous ones with which you are recognizable. Start by drawing your thoughts regarding a toxic or unwanted behavior, at that point, identify the inverse — a more advantageous characteristic that would be available in a positive relationship.

For every one of the ten toxic relationship qualities recorded below, counter with one sound relationship characteristic.

Model:

Harmful trait: brutal trustworthiness

Inverse healthy trait: honesty with damaging thought harmful

Characteristics of healthy relationships

Similarly, as specific attributes, practices, perspectives, and desires can create a toxic or damaging relationship, different qualities, practices, mentalities, and desires support sound relationships. Seven main characteristics give the structure for such sound relationships. How about we examine each:

1. Shared respect
In a sound relationship, the two participants have an essential level of respect for one another as people. At the point when you respect somebody, you treat them well.

2. Trust

Relationships thrive when each individual can trust the other.

Trust is earned, and whenever broken, the break must be repaired before the relationship can develop once more.

3. Empathy

Empathy is the acknowledgement of and concerns for someone else's pain. Empathy doesn't mean you try to fix somebody's issues for them, however, that you can care about their misery.

4. Confident communication

In a sound relationship, the two participants clearly and unmistakably inform each other of their thoughts and feelings while respecting the other individual's thoughts and feelings.

5. Agreement

In a sound relationship, the two participants are willing to proactively address struggle, cooperating to discover a commonly satisfying agreement.

6. Genuineness and authenticity

Being compassionately honest with one another allows both people to be open and real in the relationship. Realness furthers the main characteristics of trust and respect.

7. Sound boundaries

In spite of Hollywood messages like "You complete me," the best and, most grounded relationships have individuality and sound boundaries.

Connections in real life

Consider the unhealthiest or most toxic relationship in your life (past or on the other hand, present). Expound on what makes or made this relationship toxic, in detail. What toxic characteristics, behaviors, and examples do/did you see?

____

____

Now consider the most advantageous relationship you have seen or experienced. Expound in detail on what makes or made this relationship sound. What characteristics, behaviors, and examples do/did you see? What makes/made this relationship not the same as the toxic one(s)?

____

____

____

____

Relationship role models
Consider the individuals throughout your life whose relationships you respect.

These relationships could be familial, for example, among family or between a parent and child, unemotional, romantic, or competent. What do you appreciate about these relationships? What points might you want to use as a model for your own relationships?

____

____

____

____

Listening

For some survivors of abuse, one of the difficulties of building new, more advantageous relationships is figuring out how to heed their gut feelings once more. Gaslighting can be so compelling at instructing victims to accept, excuse, or then again push down their reactions to toxic behavior; they may feel unfit to understand a sound relationship by any means. At times, when the psyche is confused, the body can bring you clarity. In this activity, you will investigate ways your body informs you as to whether a relationship is sound or not.

Think about a relationship you think is harmful. Create an image of the other person in your mind, or review a memory of negative communication with that individual. Try not to go to the most noticeably awful memory you have. Rather, think of an upsetting, yet not overpowering, memory. At the point when you have the memory immovably in your psyche, answer the following questions:

What feelings do you experience when you think about this individual or collaboration?

____

____

____

What does your body feel like as you think about this individual or the relationship? Focus on your breathing (fast and shallow, or moderate and, deep?), tension in your muscles (clenched jaw or hands?), pain or strength (abrupt cerebral pain?), or different feelings (butterflies in the stomach?).

____

____

____

What sort of stance do you naturally have when you think about this individual? Would you like to twist up in a ball, hide away under the table, or raise your clenched hands?

____

____

____

____

Select a real feeling to concentrate on, for example, pretense, tension, pain, or peace. You may close your eyes, in the if you wish. Focus on the feeling, and observe what feelings come up as you focus on your body. What feelings are associated with your physical reaction?

____

____

____

____

Now consider the most beneficial relationship in your life. Fix a picture of the other individual firmly in your mind and pull up a memory of when you felt adored, supported, accepted, or thought about. What feelings come up with this memory?

____

____

____

____

What does your body feel like as you think about this individual and this relationship? Focus on your breathing, tension or unwinding in your muscles, pain or strength, and some other real feelings .

____

____

____

____

What type of stance do you instinctively hold when you think about this individual?

____

____

Select a real feeling to focus on, for example, pretense, tension, pain, or peace. You may close your eyes, if you wish. Focus on the feeling, and observe what feelings come up as you focus on your body.

What feelings are associated with your physical reaction?

____

____

____

____

What differences do you notice in the way your body reacts to a toxic relationship versus a sound one? By what method can you utilize your body's messages to examine whether a relationship is a sound?

____

____

____

____

Resetting unrealistic expectations

In some cases, an individual who has experienced numerous toxic relationships has a hard time grasping how to deal with relationship issues usefully.

With toxic friends, family, and other relationship partners, they may pardon an excessive amount of damaging behavior with the expectations that the behavior will one day stop. Or then again, they may have the reasonable—at the end of the day unrealistic— a expectation that sound relationships mean nobody gets hurt.

In all actuality, we as a whole identify with one another as imperfect, flawed people.

Mix-ups and slips up will occur. We may expect a lot of from some, and, extremely little of others. This activity allows you to examine a part of the basic unreasonable expectations that can incite hurt and disappointment in someone.

Unreasonable expectation #1: my partner will complete me as an individual.

Reasonable change #1: I am   complete without anyone else. My partner and I support one another, yet neither of us needs the other to be complete.

Ways this unreasonable expectation has appeared for me:

____

____

____

____

Unreasonable expectation #2: setting the correct boundaries will make my person in this relationship stop pleasing me so poorly.

Reasonable change #2: boundaries characterize my actions, decisions, and resistance. I can't change another person, just myself.

Ways this unreasonable expectation has appeared for me:

____

____

____

____

Unreasonable expectation #3: if my loved one is annoyed with me, I owe it to them to make them feel better.

Reasonable change #3: I am responsible for my emotions and actions, and my loved one is responsible for theirs. I can feel sympathy for my loved one's emotions without assuming the responsibility of those sentiments.

Ways this unreasonable expectation has appeared for me:

____

____

____

____

Unreasonable expectation #4: love implies never saying you're sorry. (Apologies, a love story.)

Reasonable change #4: if I genuinely hurt or wrong somebody, regardless of it being accidental, I care enough to assume responsibility and try to make it right.

Ways this unreasonable expectation has appeared for me:

____

____

____

____

Unreasonable expectation #5: an extremely sound relationship will never bring me torment.

Reasonable change #5: we are, for the most part, human, and we all make mistakes. I don't expect perfection, and I realize I will make mistakes, as well.

Ways this unreasonable expectation has appeared for me:

Sound relationship models in pop culture

A considerable lot of the relationships depicted in movies, on tv, and celebrity culture are not exactly sound. A few, be that as it may, fill in as models of sound relationships in real life. Here are some positive models:

• Ben Wyatt and Leslie Knope in parks and recreation (dating and married);

• River and Simon Tam in "Firefly and Serenity" (family);

• Cameron and Mitchell in the "Modern Family" (married);

• Elizabeth and Henry McCord in "Madam Secretary" (married);

• Ted and Marshall in "How I Met your Mother" (friends);

• Harry and Hermione in the Harry Potter books (friends);

- The hobbits in "Lord of the Rings" (friends);
- Juno and Mac in "Juno" (child and parent);
- The Johnson family in "Black-ish" (family);
- The Pearsons in "This is Us" (family);

What different models would you be able to consider? Outline with them here:

____

____

____

____

____

Sound relationship benefits

How does taking an interest in sound relationships really help you? The list below outlines some of the advantages of sound, positive relationships.
Include your own below!

- healthy relationships improve physical wellbeing.

• healthy relationships improve psychological wellness.

• healthy relationships support confidence, security, and self-esteem.

• healthy relationships allow individuals to experience and resolve clashes without hopelessly bursting the association.

• healthy relationships support individuals through noteworthy life changes, for example, births, passings, relationships, separations, and profession changes.

• healthy relationships among parents benefit kids in a family.

More advantages of sound relationships:

____

____

____

____

____

Sound relationship behaviors

Sound relationships are made through mindset, intentions, and actions. Constructing a sound relationship without acting in ways that improve wellbeing is unimaginable. The following is a list of sound relationship practices. How might you show these in your relationships?

Assuming responsibility for your own thoughts, feelings, and actions, I can show this responsibility by:

____

____

____

____

Conveying assertively

I can show these assertions by:

____

____

____

____

Taking an interest and collaborating with peers and colleagues

I can show this cooperation and a joint effort by:

____

____

____

Respecting others' boundaries

I can show this respect by:

____

____

____

____

I can show having reasonable requests by:

____

____

____

____

Being consistent and reliable

I can show this consistency and unwavering quality by:

____

____

____

Supporting loved ones

I can show this support by:

____

____

____

Demonstrating appreciation

I can show this appreciation by:

____

____

____

Supporting what you have . To create more beneficial, more grounded relationships, appreciating and supporting the ones you have is fundamentally important. A strong friendship, family relationship, work relationship, or close relationship can be a significant help as you work to recover from a toxic relationship. Don't take the individuals in your life who love and support you for granted. What are a some different ways you can sustain your positive relationships?

Get to know each other.

There is not real possible replacement for really investing energy in somebody who thinks about you. Try not to allow yourself to be "too occupied" to invest energy in friends and family. If being in a similar place really isn't a choice, find an ideal opportunity for a telephone or video call. Be careful of the urge to put off the time you put in on the grounds that you realize the other individual will consistently be there for you. relationships flourish when you put the time and energy into taking care of them.

Identify one opportunity to invest energy in a positive relationship this week.

____

____

____

____

Offer thanks and appreciation.

A really cherishing and strong relationship is worth more than gold, yet once in a while, we neglect to communicate our appreciation and thankfulness for those who have been with each of all us along. Try not to assume your friends and family know how you feel—ensure they know!

Identify one thing you can g thankfulness for in a positive relationship.

Offer your support

You may feel like you're continuously asking for help, and never   reliable enough to give it. Sound relationships depend on give-and-take, even if the giving and taking appear to be rare. Maybe one individual shows support by offering a source of genuine sympathy, while another shows support by preparing a dinner for a mournful loved one. How might you support your loved ones?

Identify one way you can offer help in a caring relationship.

____

____

____

____

____

Organize your healthy relationships

Centering the greater part of your time and energy on the relationships, you need to improve, or withdraw from can be inviting. There is a reason for putting in the time, and energy into improving a relationship by defining boundaries, communicating all the more decisively, and caring more for yourself. However, similarly, if not progressively, significant is to offer energy to ensuring solid connections flourish. Connections put on a heating surface are in danger of decay. How might you organize the connections that feed and backing you?

Identify one opportunity to establish a sound relationship this week.

____

____

____

Perceiving the patterns

All the time, the toxic relationship elements your involvement with the present have establishes in frightful past encounters. All through this activity guide, you have identified and examined the thoughts and relationship models that drove you to the toxic relationships you are presently working on recovering from. Here, you will assemble the sections to identify the cycle that has taken you back to undesirable relationships time and time again.

The relationship blueprints with which you started

Recall the relationship history exercises you finished in parts 3, 4, and 5. Use what you discovered about your family relationships, outline what you were taught about how relationships are, feel, and work. This structures the premise of the relationship design with which you began.

Model: my relationship design was watching my folks fight continuously. They attack each other, and whoever hurt the other one most was the champ. That taught me that violence was normal.

My relationship outline:

____

____

____

____

____

____

The self-concepts that make you vulnerable

Review all the activities in parts 2, 3, 4, and 5 exploring the way your thoughts about yourself have made you defenseless against gaslighting.

Summarize the thoughts you hold (or recently held) about yourself that have added to being exploited in toxic relationships.

My self-concepts:

____

____

____

____

The self-concept that keeps you stuck

In parts 3, 4, and 5, you examined how your self-observation may keep you trapped in toxic relationships. In part 6, you distinguished hindrances to self-care that may add to stagnation. Summarize how your self-concept may have kept you trapped in toxic relationships.

My self-concept:

____

____

____

____

____

The abuses you have tolerated

Toxic relationships proceed on the grounds that one group has been willing or adapted to ignore, pardon, or endure oppressive behavior. In parts 1 and 2, you learned what gaslighting is, what drives a gaslighter, and what makes gaslightees powerless against abuse. Summarize what you have discovered about abuse in your toxic relationships.

Abuse I have endured:

____

____

____

____

Breaking the cycle

Since you have identified the negative examples and patterns of your toxic relationships, it is the time to break the cycle. For each part of the toxic relationship, identify one way to break the cycle.

Model: my relationship design depended on viewing my parent fight and be violent towards one another. I can change the design by deciding to fight fair or to leave a relationship where callousness is commonplace.

Changing the blueprint

One way I can change the design is:

____

____

____

____

Checking the self-beliefs that made me vulnerable. One way I can check a self-thought that made me powerless is:

____

____

____

____

Testing the self-concept that kept me stuck. One self-thought I can challenge is:

____

____

____

____

Deciding not to accept the abuse. One way I can decide not to accept continued abuse is:

____

____

____

____

____

____

Try not to take the bait

Gaslighters keep victims trapped by causing them to accept they can't trust the soundness of their abilities. They control their victims by overruling their feeling of having been dealt with in an injurious manner, keeping them trapped in a hurtful cycle. If a victim develops enough fearlessness to remain firm and rid themselves of the toxic behavior, gaslighters may switch strategies and promise to change their behavior. Shockingly, in oppressive relationships, this promise isn't made with a legitimate prospect of self-improvement.

Or maybe, the unfilled words serve just to draw victims back into the relationship at a point where they may have broken the cycle.

In the most deep levels of the sea, there is an animal called an anglerfish that draws prey into its jaws by dangling a little, sparkling light before its teeth. Like an anglerfish attracting victims with a fake promise of light in the deep, gaslighters draw victims back in with vows to change.

How have you been drawn once more into harmful relationships throughout your life?

____

____

____

____

____

____

____

____

How can you make yourself resilient to the appeal of a fake promises?

What do you have to do to instruct yourself to combat the draw of the light?

____

____

____

____

____

Toxic behavior can be unintentional

Imagine a good scenario in which I revealed to you that toxic behavior can occur.

Oppressive goal? The truth of the matter is, not all negative relationship practices are essentially damaging. Indeed, even kind, adoring, humane individuals can participate in undesirable practices.

They may not know what they're doing.

Seeing someone that is unexpectedly pernicious, there is a reasonable possibility the other individual will show some readiness and inspiration to learn more advantageous practices.

They will respect your boundaries and acknowledge responsibility for their actions. In a toxic relationship, the other individual won't respect your limits and will accuse you.

We are largely results of our condition just as our personality . While numerous individuals may positively look to control others for their own advantage, many take part in ruins behaviors essentially in light of the fact that they don't have the foggiest idea about any other way to act. Now and again, the primary way in which we learn strong relationship practices is to endure the results of our ruinous actions.

Consider the relationships throughout your life that have been defined by unfavorable patterns and practices. Can you identify any that may have been surprisingly destructive, or controlled to damaging?

Check yourself for fleas

There is a familiar saying : "Lie with dogs, and you'll end up with fleas." Though maybe not the most beguiling expression, it has some truth to it. Over time, individuals who have been in abusive relationships may discover themselves taking part in toxic behavior themselves. Victims of abuse may feel like the best way to gain power, or to avoid being exploited again, is to turn the toxic behavior against the other individual. Be gentle, but careful, of possible insects in your own behavior.

The main part of the apology

In the event that you have been gaslit into saying "sorry" when you didn't do anything wrong, you might feel naturally hesitant to finish an activity about statements of regret. I urge you to do it, nonetheless.

Neither individual in a sound relationship, as we have recently talked about, can totally avoid making mistakes and hurting their partner. Realizing when and how to make an earnest apology is key to making and sustaining sound relationships.

A viable apology is:

- Convenient. A decent apology is offered at the right time. It is better, to apologize sooner than later; if you find out later that you hurt somebody, offer the statement of apology as soon as you discover that you have.
- Earnest. "Sorry/not heartbroken" isn't a statement of regret. Nor is "I'm grieved, be that as it may, " offer a statement of regret earnestly and truly, without attempting to excuse or validate your actions.
- Required in instances of genuine bad behavior or harm. An apology isn't essential when you have not really done anything wrong.

Gaslighters will try to make you apologize for things that are not your responsibility. Try not to take the bait.

You were focused on your own activities. In the event that you have accomplished something that wrongs or hurts someone else, center your expression of remorse around what you did.

____

____

____

____

Quite a bit of this exercise manual has been centered around helping you modify your relationship with yourself. Gaslighting isolates you from your feeling of self and makes you doubt yourself. So, to make more beneficial relationships moving forward, you should first rebuild the relationship you have with yourself.

Review your thought practices in part 6. Similarly, as you have to put energy into sustaining sound relationships so they can flourish, you need to put energy into reestablishing your relationship with yourself. Write a letter to yourself, a letter of assurance, talk about your expectation to rediscover, sustain, and extend your relationship with yourself. You value your own affection, care, compassion, and responsibility.

My letter of commitment:

____

____

Sound relationship affirmation

Create three mantras to call abundance of sound relationships into your life. Make sure to talk with certainty that you will get what you are looking for.

Models:

I am appreciative of the love and support I receive in my relationships.

I value the individuals around me, who care for me and build me up.

I invite happiness and growth in my relationships.

Your turn:

Review and wrap-up. Look back at the activities in this section.

What impacted you the most?

____

____

____

____

What didn't resound with you?

____

____

____

____

How do you feel as of now? Have your sentiments changed since you began this section?

____

____

____

____

What will you take away from these activities?

CONCLUSION

Congrats on finishing the gaslighting recovery book! In working through these activities, you have stepped toward a more advantageous life. A few sections and activities were likely harder than others; you ought to be glad for yourself for working through them. If there were any activities or areas you found excessively troublesome or difficult to work through, I urge you to try again with the help of an advisor. Keep in mind: seeking help is definitely not an indication of weakness, but the clear declaration that you need some additional help.

I wish I could state that finishing this exercise manual all your relationships will from this time forward be sound, satisfying, and fulfilling.

Tragically, I can't make that guarantee. Be that as it may, I can say that by working through these activities, you have made the opportunities for development, change, and recovery as well as a chance of an entirely different life.

Because of your work to recover and recuperate, you will walk into new relationships with a changed feeling of your value and worth. You will be all the more able to expect reasonable treatment, and more averse to fall prey to harmful individuals. If you do end up in a harmful relationship, you will be better prepared to withdraw and end the cycle. You will be better ready to practice self-care, self-compassion, and self-consideration.

I am so pleased with you, dear reader, for your devotion to your recovery what's more, healing. You are strong, and fearless. You are valuable—and are equipped for making—loving, strong, and sound relationships. Good karma to you as you start the following part of your life feeling more grounded, more sure, and all the more entirely you.

I wish you fulfillment, hope, and recovery.